MW00879894

MANIC KINGDOM

By
Dr. Erin Stair

Based on a true story

Published by Gray Productions
Guttenberg, New Jersey

Published by Gray Productions
212-315-2449
JudyCorc@aol.com
www.judycorcoran.com

ISBN-10: 198403295X
ISBN-13: 978-1984032959
Book and cover design by Judy Corcoran
Printed in January 2018

This book is dedicated to
all those who question systems
and believe in second chances.

Manic Kingdom is a true story — that is, true to my memory. For a variety of reasons, however, it is not completely nonfiction. I changed names, even my name and the name of my cat. Names of institutions, schools and hospitals have been omitted or changed, because they aren't relevant, and some of the scenes involve sensitive medical and private information. Dialogue is not verbatim and some events and timelines have been altered or compressed. Believe it or not, some of the more provocative scenes were left out.

While the overall theme of the epilogue true, it is a fictional scene.

PART I

1

I have a hunch that Chase is going through something. Med school takes its toll on all of us and many people don't make it or need psychiatric medication to get them through. It's sort of like military training. Some can cut it, some can't, and some go crazy. Everyone expected me to do well. My older sister tried to help, by giving me this advice: *Try not to be weird.*

She went on: *Blend in, make friends, and don't be all Emily Dickinson-ish. Talk to normal people and make normal friends. Maybe you'll meet a nice, normal guy. And don't make too many jokes. Guys don't date the class clown. This is the beginning of an amazing experience for you.*

And it was. I'm more than half-way through my second year of med school, with the finish line in sight, and her words haunt me—now more than ever. Looking back, I wish I had taken her advice.

I remember my first few days well, as Chase was a big

part of it. I was standing by myself in the middle of the school lobby, where groups of new students were getting to know each other after a painful two-hour slide presentation on what to expect in medical school. They were planning parties, shopping trips, bar crawls and already forming study groups. I was clutching the straps of my black backpack and staring at the circles of excited doctors-to-be. The circles were tight. I wondered how I could break in, as if it were a game of Red Rover instead of normal socialization. I looked cute in a cheap, but flattering, black sun dress and sandals, but the circles didn't seem to notice. Maybe I didn't look cute, maybe I looked weird. The dress was kind of Goth and unprofessional. I must have looked weird, because I felt weird.

Then I saw a guy who looked weirder than me. He was wearing a baggy, button-down, tan shirt and khaki pants and standing behind a plant in the corner of the lobby. His eyes were soft and brown and went well with his olive skin and dark frothy hair. I noticed him because he looked older than the other students, and because he looked like a scared puppy hiding from a thunderstorm. I decided he wasn't bad-looking, but he looked too pathetic to be attractive. He was definitely not the nice, normal guy my sister had in mind. As if hopelessly committed to weirdness, I decided to introduce myself.

On my way over to him, I noticed he had a sheet of toilet

paper sticking out of the backside of his pants. A circle with ten pairs of eyes kept looking at him and laughing. He was definitely not getting in the circle.

I stepped in front of him and the plant. "Hi! I'm Becka. You are...?"

He tensed up and looked at me with utter surprise, or maybe borderline horror. I almost regretted approaching him. Then his shoulders relaxed and he stuttered, "Oh...Hi. I'm Chase. Nice to, uh, meet you."

"Chase. Can I tell you something?"

"Uh, sure?" He laughed nervously.

I leaned in closer and whispered in his ear. "You have a piece of T-P stickin' out of your pants."

He backed away from me. His jaw dropped and his eyes bulged as he reached behind him and smacked the small of his back. Horrified at what he touched, he muttered, "Oh my God." The color red hijacked his face.

I felt guilty and second-guessed myself; maybe I shouldn't have told him.

"You know," I started, completely ignoring the laughing med students at my side, "it's really not that noticeable. I've done stuff like this before. Once, I went outside and forgot to put on a shirt."

Chase looked horrified again. Then his face softened, and he blew out a laugh. Phew! He was still with me, so I continued, "Yeah, I was changing out of my bathing suit when

I overheard some guy talkin' smack about me outside on the porch. Man, I got pissed. I stormed out of the bathroom and just started yellin' at him. A bunch of people were around, including my grandpa. It was beyond embarrassing."

"Wow. That's...quite a story. How old were you?"

I was nine. "Nineteen," I lied. He chuckled and relaxed a little. I could tell he felt better.

"Hey," he said nervously while glancing around the lobby. "There, um...there are no marks on there, are there?"

"Oh, the T-P?" I feigned cluelessness. "Well, I can't really see from this angle, but I don't think so."

That conversation is how Chase and I started our own circle, though we probably only looked like a half-circle.

A few nights later, Chase and I met at the school's welcoming party at a popular Philadelphia bar and sat alone at a small table in the corner. When we weren't chatting, we listened to the music and stared at the hive of drunk and almost-drunk classmates swarming the dance floor. Chase told me he was Italian, thirty-five years old, and worked as an actor and comedian in New York City before deciding on med school. He had a knack for imitating cartoon characters and political figures. I told him a few of my own jokes, but not enough to be labeled the class clown.

Our conversation was interrupted by Trevor, a short, muscular, frat boy from Florida, fresh off the conveyer belt from the Meat-Head Factory. His bleached blonde hair and shiny veneers made me want to put on my sunglasses. I sensed he was used to picking up women and having his way with them.

"Becka, right?" he asked, while sitting down in an empty chair at our table.

"Yep. That's me," I responded coldly. I glanced over at Chase, gripped my beer can, and shifted my seat farther away from Trevor.

"I heard you went to a military school for college. And played soccer there? That's so cool! We were all just talking about it over there. It's kinda weird for a girl, though. Are you like a lesbian?" Trevor asked confidently and sincerely.

I looked down and chuckled at his audacity. I was a perfect stranger and his question was personal. Still, I was aware that his misconception was fairly common; a lot of civilians assumed women in the military were gay, or at the least, butch and unattractive. It was an ignorant stereotype that, like so many other stupid things, insisted on existing. I used to get offended, but after a while it simply amused me. I decided to toy with him a bit.

"Why do you ask?"

Trevor looked stumped, as if he was sure I'd answer affirmatively. We stared at each other for a few long seconds, when Chase intervened.

"Actually, Becka was just telling me that being a lesbo

is a requirement for military school. There was one box on the application that required more than a checkmark, if you catch my drift," Chase said with a wink.

We both laughed. Napoleon Bonaparte looked confused, like we had just poked a hole in his balloon of an ego. He mumbled, "Later," and walked towards the dancing swarm. Still laughing, I realized then that Chase and I were going to be great friends.

Eventually we became roommates. We studied together, ate together, played pranks on each other and did everything but sleep together. He was the reason I didn't fail Gross Anatomy. Chase immediately recognized my anxiety over cutting up cadavers and called my bluff when I told him I was allergic to the smell of formaldehyde. He forced me to the lab with him three nights a week and turned dissection of the dead into a game. It was outrageously disrespectful, but it was emotional survival. It was the only way I passed.

Outside school, our apartment was a quirky, fun place, but I have a sinking feeling that it will all end. Lately, Chase has been annoying me with random questions, and he's looking behind things, around things and under things, like he's always on a scavenger hunt. A lot of it has to do with Matthew, another classmate, who quickly became my boyfriend.

It still feels weird to call Matthew that. He's a former

musician, six years older than me and blessed with model looks: chiseled physique, green eyes, chestnut hair, and a smile that makes flowers face him. We get along great, but something about our relationship feels superficial. Most of the time, I feel like I'm acting, just going through the motions and not the emotions. We've been together for nearly two years, but maybe we don't see each other enough for the relationship to grow deeper. There isn't a lot of spare time for romance during med school. Most days are burdened by the pressure to study and get good grades.

Still, Matthew and I squeeze in a proper date when we can. We see movies, we take day trips to Lancaster and gawk at the Amish, and we go to concerts. I've even met his parents. We managed to label ourselves "boyfriend and girlfriend," mostly because we had hung out enough times and figured that's what we were supposed to do. He told me he loved me a month ago, and I said I loved him, too, but even that felt weird. It felt like my mouth was constipated. I had to strain to get the words out.

But today is Saturday and I'm looking forward to seeing Matthew tonight, as sort of a reward for studying. I'm currently in the school library, where I've been for the last seven hours or so. I'm in a baggy, comfy navy blue jogging suit, my typical marathon-studying outfit, and stretching by my cubicle. My highlighted pathology book is open on the desk in front of me, begging for my attention. As I lunge back and forth, I scold myself that I can't spend one more second thinking about Matthew, Chase or anyone for that matter. I have a huge test next week, possibly the biggest one before third year. Still, my mind isn't absorbing knowledge. I wish it were a sponge, but it's more like a bouncy ball. Bounce, bounce, away from all these depressing diseases. While lunging, I accidentally knock my chair over. The girl in the adjacent cubicle shoots me a murderous look under a mane of greasy hair. She's been here as long as I have, and it's the first time I've seen her face. To avoid a budding confrontation with my cubicle neighbor, I decide to go for a walk with the hope of finding motivation along the way.

Past the lobby, I walk into the bathroom. All of the stalls are occupied. Unpleasant sounds and putrid smells linger in the stagnant air. I try to breathe only through my mouth. Irritable bowel, I think to myself—all these Type-A med students and their suffering, slimy intestinal loops.

The mirror beckons me because it will waste time. I stand in front of it and evaluate myself. My long, brown hair is cinched in a messy ponytail. My face looks puffy. I need to wax my bushy eyebrows; they're starting to look like pubes. The lines between my luminous blue eyes look more prominent than usual. I scold myself; it's all that damn brow furrowing. I need to start rubbing castor oil on my face which I hear works for wrinkles. My skin looks extra pale, and I should have put on eye makeup. I suck in my belly, look at myself from the side, and then let it go. I'm on the small side but will never admit it. Some days I think I look pretty, but today is not one of those days.

Someone flushes and a stall is free. I pee while listening to two classmates, one Indian and one Caucasian, discuss our upcoming exam. They brag about their study strategies. They're excited. They love this stuff. Sitting on the toilet, listening, I feel like a weird, lost intruder.

2

"Where are you going this late?" Chase asks as I put on my coat, after spending all day studying and knowing I need a break. I don't answer and instead reach for the doorknob, but he body blocks me and asks again.

"Matthew's," I say with some annoyance in my voice. "Where I always go, Chase. Is something wrong?"

"No." He fidgets, still in my space. "Becka, are you... are you a prostitute?" he blurts out accusingly.

I feel my forehead lift as my eyes lunge forward. Chase remains motionless against our apartment's cracked, anemic wall. His arms are loosely crossed over a baggy, stained white t-shirt that covers a pair of ripped and grungy jeans. Barefoot and dirty, I assume he hasn't showered in days. I giggle and start tugging on my hair.

"Well? Are you?" Chase asks again. His voice is louder now, and he doesn't sound like he's joking. I want to run out the door but my knees feel locked. I can feel my insides waiting—no, begging—for the punch-line. Drops of sweat slide down my stomach. I cautiously rub them off with my sweatshirt. I don't want to startle him.

"Answer me, Becka!" he yells, smacking his hand against the wall.

I cringe as if he hit me instead. "Why would you ask me that, Chase?" I ask softly. "I go to Matthew's all the time. He's my boyfriend. You know this."

Chase doesn't budge. I can feel him studying me. He stares at some part of my body, but I don't know which. I refuse to look straight at his eyes. Eyes paralyze people with the truth, and I need to move. He furrows his brow and answers. "Because you always go out at night, Becka, and never come home. Do you think I don't notice? I live here too! I always notice!"

I watch as he exhales with his mouth closed, making his cheeks puff out. He looks like he's pouting.

"Chase, I have a boyfriend. I sleep at Matthew's. Why are you asking me this? You know this!" I say rapidly and loudly. "For Christ's sake, Chase, if I were getting paid for sex do you think I'd be living in this dump?"

With each word, I feel my courage building. Instead of running away, I want to push him. He needs to leave me the hell alone, so I can go.

Then our eyes connect and I can't look away. My neck is useless, as if the histrionic, instigating universe has locked our heads in place. His eyes reveal things I don't want to see:

Chase, but not Chase. Chase is not in those eyes. They look like two pools of aggressive quicksand and if I stare too long, I'll get sucked into his mad world. I'm half tempted to hold up a crucifix.

Chase sighs, looks down, skulks into his bedroom, and slams the door shut.

My left arm starts shaking, then my right. More sweat slides down my body as my nerves fire shots of adrenaline to remind me I'm still alive. With Chase now out of view, I feel like I've been hallucinating. I reach for the doorknob but stop. An aching deep inside me halts my hand. I want to make sure Chase is okay. I want the old Chase back. I want to knock on his door, go into his bedroom, and rescue my friend.

But I don't. I leave to see Matthew.

Matthew takes me to bed as soon as I get there. I fake an orgasm and we both fall asleep. I wake up earlier than he does, dress in yesterday's clothes, and quietly sneak out to the school library to study there all day. Even at eight o'clock on a Sunday morning the library is saturated with med students, all shoved into tiny spaces and hovering over piles of lecture notes. Most cubicles are already taken, but luckily I find an empty one near the back. I inhale deeply, overcome by the scent of strong coffee, the aroma of work.

Studying doesn't start well. My pathology book is open to a chapter on lymphomas. I try reading a page, but nothing sticks. The glossy pictures of swollen, diseased lymph nodes don't help, nor do my various brightly colored highlighters. It's tough because the nature of the material is gloomy and morbid, a complete antithesis to the sunny day outside. It's disease after disease, ad infinitum. Abnormal cells, malignant lumps, blocked vessels, yellow skin, crusty ulcers and green discharges. It's death and dying every day, all day, so much so that I feel like medical school robs me of my naive youth. All this mortality stuff should be reserved for old people, not young. It makes me want to burn my books. It makes me want to scream, drink, eat fattening foods, go to an amusement park and get a tattoo.

I sigh and remind myself that it's the biggest test of the year. All I have to do is take the test, take my Boards, and start clinicals. Then I'll be done.

I study for all of fifteen minutes. My eyes drift up and away from the page. More students are in the library now. They are swimming in their studies. Their brains are storing buzz words that will get them high scores on our upcoming test. No one seems bothered. No one seems to mind memorizing all the death stuff. All of them are just computers, contentedly storing data.

I think of Matthew and wonder where he's studying. I wonder why he never invites me to study with him. Probably because he actually studies.

3

Monday, test day, has arrived. For five hours I struggle through my pathology exam, a mixture of multiple choice questions and essays. My hand aches from writing, my stomach is growling and my head feels like someone is tightening a band around it. Med school feels like a marathon for your brain. After I turn in the exam, I wish that I had studied more. I always wish that, and it never happens.

A couple of my classmates invite me to a local deli for an after-test meal. I decline. The last thing I want to do now is listen to intense, Type-A students compare exam answers. Plus, I have a rescheduled session with Dr. Brown for this afternoon. I jump in my Jeep and drive to his office on the Mainline. For the last four months, I have been shadowing Dr. Brown. My school paired me with him as part of its program to prepare students for their clinical years. At eighty-two, he moves slowly and hesitantly, like he's always surrounded by caution tape.

"Come in!" he yells, holding his hand over the

mouthpiece of the phone, his voice old and raspy.

I nearly trip over a stack of magazines on the floor as I enter. Dr. Brown motions me toward a dusty chair covered in books. I smile, pick up the books one by one, carefully place them on the floor, and sit. His office is a broken hip waiting to happen. It looks as if every medical journal published in the last fifty years is here. He hangs up the phone and smiles.

"Well, Becka, we have to go to the hospital today to see a few folks. Shouldn't take too long. Why don't you wait for me by my car?"

I stroll out to the parking lot and stand by his shiny, black Lexus, which is parked next to my Jeep. My stomach growls so I dig through my purse for something to eat. I find a stale, half-melted energy bar. It's been in there for weeks. I bite off a piece as Dr. Brown wobbles down the sidewalk from the clinic to his car. He's wearing a cap and carrying a black, leather bag in his left hand.

He pushes a button on his key-fob and the Lexus unlocks automatically. I slide easily into the passenger seat and wipe away crumbs from my white blouse and black pants. Dr. Brown lowers himself into the driver's seat at a geological pace. He softly moans and lets out small gasps of air, as if moving each joint and flexing each muscle is painful. Once he's situated behind the wheel, he turns the ignition and squints out the windshield. I'm not sure he can see. I may die, I think to myself as I buckle the seatbelt across my torso.

He points us toward the freeway, and I calculate the hospital is about twenty minutes away.

"How's school going for you?" he asks.

I wonder if this is small talk or whether he's genuinely interested. "Okay. Had a test today. Not sure how I did yet." We putter down the freeway as aggressive Philadelphia drivers fly by us.

"What made you choose med school in the first place?"

I'm surprised. He's never asked me about my motivations before. Maybe he's mentally writing my evaluation form already.

"Um...to help people." My answer feels flat. I silently and sarcastically scold myself. It couldn't have been more pathetic or cliché. But what was I supposed to tell him? That when I was growing up, my mother used acts of terror to convince my two sisters and me that there were only two careers in this world: McDonald's and medicine. That getting a grade lower than an A-plus gave her chest pains because it put me one step closer to mopping whoppers and one step away from being a doctor, the only career that mattered? That until I got to college, I thought there were only two majors I could choose from, chemistry and Mickey Mouse, and if I picked Mickey Mouse I might as well not go to college? Should I have said that? How about that after four years in a military school, thinking only about killing people, I needed to think about healing people? Should I mention that I feel lost on the inside, I'm only doing what I think I'm smart enough to do and supposed to do? Would that have been a better answer? Okay, I'm being histrionic and negative. I could talk about how I enjoy helping people and taking care of them...but I'm getting sick of taking care of people who don't take care of themselves. Okay, I'm being negative again. I'll just be quiet.

After my pointless internal debate, I glance over at Dr. Brown. I can't be sure, but his eye lids look droopy. The car feels like it's going slower, which I didn't think was possible. Oh my God! He's falling asleep on the Interstate! My heart flutters. I reach down and turn up the radio. Trombones suddenly rock the inside of his car. Horns so loud, I feel like they're in my head. I stare wide-eyed at Dr. Brown, looking for a reaction. Nothing. The man is asleep.

I talk louder. "IT'S A REAL PASSION OF MINE, DR. BROWN. MEDICINE. YES, I LOVE IT! I ABSOLUTELY LOVE IT AND EVERYTHING IT STANDS FOR! TO FIRST DO NO HARM. THAT'S BEAUTIFUL!"

I'm not even sure what I'm screaming. Just words. His right eyelid lifts a little. I should shove him. Is that disrespectful? Shoving your preceptor? Screw it. He's going to crash the car, and with my luck, I won't die. I'll end up a vegetable.

I lightly shove the meat of his right, upper arm with my palm. Both of his eyes pop open. He's awake.

"That's good. That's really good," he murmurs. I'm not sure what he's responding to, but I don't care.

Dr. Brown turns on his signal. I look out the window and sigh with relief as the hospital comes into sight.

After entering through the hospital's front doors, I excuse myself to the ladies' room. Dr. Brown nods and promises to wait for me. Once inside the bathroom, I dial Matthew's number. "Hi babe. Listen, I hate to ask, but can you do me a huge favor?" I plead.

"What?" he asks. I detect slight annoyance.

"Can you pick me up from the hospital? My preceptor fell asleep at the wheel and he drove me here. Please? In like an hour? Please?"

Matthew sighs. "Becka, I really have to study. You really think he fell asleep?"

"Yes! You don't even have to drive me back to his office where my car is. Just to home. Chase will take me to my car later. Please? He falls asleep!" I'm shouting into the receiver. "You're supposed to be my boyfriend, Matthew! You can't come pick me up when I'm telling you I might die if I go home with this man? Fine. Whatever."

"No, I didn't say that. I just have a lot of work to do. Okay, I'll pick you up." Matthew concedes, but his tone says that the last thing he wants to do is pick me up. Normally, my pride would urge me to hang up immediately and ignore him for a week, but right now I'm too afraid of dying in

Brown's Lexus.

"That's fine," I reply coldly, and hang up.

Back in the lobby, Dr. Brown smiles at me as we walk over to the elevator and rise to the sixth floor. "I figure we'll start in the ICU. I have three patients in there," he informs me. The elevator door opens, and we're in the ICU.

Nurses with tired, overworked faces, dressed in pink and blue scrubs, scurry around the unit. They hurry between patients' bedsides, while monitors haunt the room with shrill asynchronous beeps. The death tones, as I call them, always make my heart rate speed up. A few serious-looking doctors write indecipherable notes in patients' charts behind the nurses' station. Chronic, oozing bed ulcers, acidic breath, poop-filled colostomy pouches, hospital-issued food trays, pointless floral arrangements combine, and the room smells like death.

Dr. Brown lightly touches my arm, mentions three patients' names, and asks me to fetch their charts. I find the large, purple, paper binders, hug them to my chest and follow Dr. Brown into his first patient's room.

A half-smiling, morbidly obese woman sits up in her hospital bed. She greets us vaguely. The doctor asks how she's feeling and she mentions an odd sensation in her calf. Dr. Brown pushes up the end of her bed sheet and examines her calves. As he gently palpates her enormous, scaly lower legs, I read in her chart that she's a Type 2 Diabetic, in the hospital for a hyperosmolar hyperglycemic crisis. Her earlier notes suggest that she's been non-compliant in following a strict diabetic diet. I look at her again. She's huge. It makes sense. Her fat rolls suggest that she inhales sweets, fats and high fructose corn syrup regularly. Sugar will eventually kill her, because she can't say no. No one can save her but herself. I sigh. Dr. Brown takes her chart from my arms and writes an order for a Doppler exam to rule out deep vein thrombosis.

His second patient is a frail, yellowish old man with chronic lung and liver issues. He's either sleeping or dead, I'm not entirely sure. Dr. Brown listens to the man's heart, writes briefly in the chart, and we move on.

The next room contains a woman, or rather, the remnants of a woman. Her lank hair, laying motionless on her pillow, is crusted with a greenish gunk. She's unconscious. Her pale, limp body is attached to a ventilator, which appears to be the only thing binding her to Earth. Her sister, a blonde haired, middle-aged woman, wearing a yellow sweater, slacks and a necklace with a cross, sits beside the bed showing a calm face. She's used to seeing her sister this way.

Without warning, the patient leans forward slightly in her bed. With her eyes still closed, she spews green and black bile out of her mouth, splattering her hospital gown and hair. She falls back against her bed. Her sister grabs tissues off a table in the room and begins wiping around the patient's mouth. My mouth opens and won't close. My heart is galloping. I feel like I just witnessed an exorcism.

"Should I call someone?" Like a priest. I have no idea what just happened, but it looked bad.

"No, no." Dr. Brown calmly waves me off. "It's a reflex. She has done that frequently now for the last month and a half."

I can't believe it. She's been like this for a month and a half?

"It's horrible to see, I know," the sister says, now tearful. She caresses the woman's forehead with her hand. "But I just can't pull the plug. Not now. I don't think she'd want that. That's not what she wanted, and I couldn't live with myself if I did that."

"Becka," Dr. Brown interrupts my reverie. I was wondering if the sister knew she'd be pulling the plug on a Brussels sprout. "Why don't you go down to Room 311 and see Mr. Cruz? You saw him as an outpatient before. Just write a quick progress note in his chart, and then you can leave." I assume he wants to talk privately to Linda Blair's sister. I am more than happy to leave.

On the elevator to the third floor, I think about death and the sister's refusal to let her sister die. There are so many machines that can keep people alive indefinitely. The thought terrifies me. Everyone's narcissistic, that's the problem. That's why death isn't as naturally accepted as being born. I want to bolt out of the hospital and drink, but I know I can't. I want to be a doctor, I think, but I question whether I can stand all the physical ugliness of it.

The elevator chimes. I walk down the busy third-floor hallway full of nurses and resident physicians to Mr. Cruz's room. His door is open and he's sitting up in bed. He's a rail-thin, ancient Hispanic man with bright sarcastic eyes. I knock, but he ignores me. I enter anyway.

"Hi, Mr. Cruz! How ya feelin'?" I try to sound chipper while I survey him from head to… knee. His right leg is missing from the knee down. His left leg had been amputated previously due to complications from a long history of uncontrolled diabetes, but his absent right leg is news to me.

"Terrible!" he mumbles angrily. "I lost my other leg. How'd you feel if you lost a leg?"

Like shit. But I keep that to myself. "Yes, I see. I didn't realize you were in here to get your other leg amputated. Sorry. Really, sorry. Other than that, are you feeling okay?" That feels like a pitiful question to ask a man who just had two legs cut off.

"No. I'm starving! They don't feed ya in here. It's awful," he complains, grimacing. "You're a good girl. Can you do me a favor while you're here? Can ya go into the third drawer there and get me my food? It should be under my socks." He gestures toward his chest of drawers. I frown, but walk over and pull open the drawer. I push his socks aside and discover two containers of Chinese food, a bag of chips, and a box of cupcakes.

Here's a diabetic who lost both his legs because he didn't follow a strict diet, and now he's asking me for illegal food hiding under his socks that he doesn't need since he lost his feet in two amputation surgeries paid for by Medicaid...I catch my breath.

"Who in God's green earth is smuggling you food?" I demand, giving zero effort to cover my surprise. "And why do you even have socks?"

"My cousin, praise the Lord. He knows they don't feed me in here," he declares crossly.

I sigh, defeated, and hand him the Chinese food and a plastic fork. He sniffs the food and digs in. I surrender. All I can do is watch.

"Well," I start, after two minutes of useless gawking, "what else could they amputate, anyway?"

He stares at me, hard. I stare back. Then I blush.

"Like hell!" he scoffs with a mouthful of fried rice, and I have to laugh. At least he can make me laugh.

Five minutes later, I step out of the elevator into the lobby and see Matthew's car parked out front, right where he said he'd be. I pray he hasn't had to wait long.

4

Matthew sees me approaching his black Toyota Celica. He leaves the car running, hops out and opens the passenger door for me. I interpret this as a good sign. Being polite means he can't be too annoyed, but then I remember he always opens doors for me. He looks bothered but he's smiling. I weakly smile back, stand on tip-toes, and kiss his lips. He pecks mine back. It feels wrong.

I slip in the passenger seat. He closes the door quickly, walks around the back of the car and gets in the driver's seat. He looks crunched up and uncomfortable. I've told him he should buy a bigger car.

"You have a ride back to your Jeep?" His fingers rapidly tap against the steering wheel.

I look at his tapping fingers. Then I look at him. He averts his eyes, stares out the windshield, out into the parking lot. Something is really wrong.

"Yes," I whisper back. My stomach feels like a honey jar being swarmed by aggressive bees. I might vomit.

He hits the gas, pulls out of the hospital lot, and turns on the radio. A song I'm unfamiliar with is playing. We drive in verbal silence as a sinking sensation takes me hostage. My body tenses as he stops abruptly at a red light. I try to grin at him, but I can't. Is he angry at me?

He turns onto the driveway leading to my apartment and stops in front of my complex but leaves the car running.

"You don't want to come in?" I sheepishly ask. My gut already knows the answer. It knows what's coming. I try to mentally brace myself, but it's useless.

Matthew starts to speak, then hesitates. I feel the emptiness of the parking lot filled with empty cars.

"Becka," he softly starts, putting his hand on top of mine. It's warm and sweaty. "Becka, I just don't think we can do this anymore. I love you, I do. But… I just don't think this is going to work out. It feels…well, sometimes it feels like we're both acting. It doesn't feel right."

He's saying what I've felt, almost exactly what I've thought, but for some reason my eyes tear up and my ears start burning. My core feels like it's caving in, and I don't understand why. I don't understand why it hurts so much.

"Why?" I manage to squeak out. "Is it something I did? Are you angry at me? Is it someone else? It's okay if you met someone else, but just tell me." My voice is shaky, nasal. A tear slides down my cheek and Matthew wipes it away with his thumb. I wish he'd be an asshole instead of being so kind.

It would make this easier.

"No, it's not someone else. And no, it's not something you did. I just… I haven't felt right about this for a while. God, I don't want to hurt you, but I can't… I don't want to be in a relationship right now." He sounds impatient. He wants to leave. He's over me.

More tears come, and my nose feels clogged. A small part of my mind reminds me that I want this too, I know this is the right thing for both of us, we are wrong for each other, and I'm upset because he's rejecting me and not the other way around. And yet, my body refuses to listen. I can't listen to him reject me. It hurts, physically. My insides feel a thousand pinpricks, like hypodermic needles. Suddenly I want him more than ever, but I know I can't sound desperate. I don't want him to think I can't live without him, even though right now, it feels like the truth.

I pull my hand out from under his and wipe my eyes. He tries to wipe another tear away but I stop him. "Well, fine. I guess I can't do anything about it. I…we'll be friends? Can we still hang out?" I'm blubbering like an idiot.

"Of course we can. I'll always be your friend," he says. He sounds cliché, and I hate him for it.

"You did meet someone else, though, I can tell. I can just feel it." I'm not even sure why I'm accusing him.

Matthew's eyes narrow and he tenses his face. He's getting frustrated. "I have had my head turned, sure. But no,

I'm not seeing anyone else."

I feel vindicated for a moment, except the thought of him being with another woman makes me want to be with him more than ever. I want him, even though I know I'll never be in love with him.

"Fine. Whatever. You could have told me earlier." I unlock the passenger door and move to exit. I can't be in this space anymore.

"Are you going to be okay?" he asks. His eyes are soft, concerned. I hate him. I hate that he got the upper hand.

"You just dumped me in a parking lot. I'm fucking fine," I snap. I slam the door and stalk to my apartment complex. I don't look back.

I'm weeping by the time the elevator doors open and I walk slowly and pitifully to my apartment, confused as to why I'm so upset. I unlock the door and step inside where I'm blinded by smoke. I start coughing violently and my eyes water. There's never been this much smoke before, but Chase has stopped going to class and it seems he spends all day chain-smoking in his bedroom.

I knock on his door, but there's no answer. I quietly open the door and peek inside. The details of his bedroom are hard to discern through the blue-ish fog. I see my cat Moses napping on Chase's window sill. I ignore my asthma and plunge in, snatching her up. Her dark fur reeks, and her eyes are foggy and confused.

Chase, wearing only his boxers, is sitting on his futon with his legs up on his coffee table. He's typing furiously on his computer, like he's in a trance. There's a lit cigarette between his fingers.

"You weren't at school today," I note. I hope to start a benign conversation. I'll save the much-needed discussion about his smoking for another time.

"I know," he responds flatly.

He's so skinny. I can see more of his ribs this week than last. He takes another drag while I wonder when he last ate.

"We had a test, you know."

"I know. I'll make it up."

"So, what are you doing?" I can't see his computer screen through the smoke.

"Stock market stuff!" he snaps, and finally turns to face me. "Becka, are you...crying?"

I nod, and clutch Moses tighter to my chest. I didn't think he'd notice.

"Why?" he asks gently. I catch a glimpse of his old, nurturing self in those tender eyes. It's a brief glimpse, but it soothes me like nothing else could at that moment.

Through shivers and sniffles, I manage a reply. "It's... Matthew, he...Matthew broke up with me!" Instantly I'm crying again. "And, I left my car at the doctor's office, and now I need a ride to my car, and I saw all this terrible stuff at the hospital, and it's just...it's all so bad! I can't believe he dumped me."

Chase stands up from his computer, grabs a box of tissues and hands them to me. "Don't cry. I'm so sorry, don't cry. You were too good for him anyway. I'll give you a ride to your car right now, okay?"

I nod, but even after I put Moses down and blow my nose, I'm still sobbing.

Chase tilts his head and smiles softly. "If it makes you feel any better, I haven't had a date in ten years. I'm the one who should be crying."

I can't help it; even with snot running down my face, I have to laugh. This is the old Chase, just when I need him most.

He puts on his sandals and dangles his car keys in front of me. I nod and follow him into the hallway. For a few moments at least, I don't think about how wrong Matthew and I felt together. I can only think about how natural it feels to be near Chase. This version of him, anyway.

5

It's been three days since Matthew dumped me. I'm spending more time at home, and Chase is back to being weird and anti-social. I'm glued to the kitchen table, studying gruesome medical knowledge for my upcoming Board exam, while Chase remains locked in his smoky bedroom. I haven't seen him all day.

As the hours drag on, I find myself losing focus and thinking more and more about Matthew. I decide to distract myself by going to the grocery store. It's approaching dinner time and there's not much in the apartment to eat. As I grab my jacket, Chase's bedroom door whips open. I jump, startled.

"Where are you going? It's late."

"Huh? I'm going to the store. I'm hungry. Do you want something to eat?" I try to steer the conversation into safe territory, but I sound nervous anyway. I can feel my heart speed up. Lately, it feels more dangerous inside my apartment instead of out.

"No. Not hungry," he answers in a staccato tone. "You left your phone on the kitchen table last night when you went to bed. It was ringing nonstop, so I answered it. Some guy named Troy? He said he was a bouncer and you guys were friends. What's that all about?"

I back away from Chase as my posture stiffens. He's interrogating me.

"Troy is a bouncer. I probably gave him my number once, a while ago, when I was drunk. I'm not friends with him, not really. He probably drunk-dialed me. It's nothing. I'm actually happy you answered the phone instead of me. Maybe he'll think I have a boyfriend and stop calling!" I giggle. I sound almost desperate for Chase to believe me, but I've told him the truth. Hearing that Troy called makes me regret giving him my number. One more stupid decision fueled by alcohol.

Chase doesn't look convinced. His stare says he's just found me guilty of some horrible, unnamed deed. "Becka! Will you just stop? Please, tell me, and for once be honest. Are you a prostitute?"

I'm insulted. The idea that I could ever be a hooker is at least amusing enough to keep me calm, but he's really starting to annoy me.

"Chase, I have no idea why you're asking me this or what's wrong with you, but no, I'm not. Would you please stop asking me that now? You're starting to piss me off," I bark at him.

I want to scream at him but I don't want to fight, so I turn around and twist the door knob. Chase jumps behind me and firmly grasps my wrist. It's slightly painful. I feel his heavy breathing against my cheek and my innards freeze solid. I'm a helpless icicle about to break.

"Don't leave me like this, Becka. Please...don't leave me like this." He's begging. His tone is so pathetic that I start to cry. I've lost the hilarious, carefree man I adore. I don't know who this person is standing in his place.

I pull my wrist free from his grip and, in between tears, plead with him, "What is wrong with you?" Then it dawns on me. "Wait...did you fall in love with me or something? Are you in love with me?"

He looks hurt and stunned and I wish I could take those words back. The question sort of fell out of my mouth. Chase and I have never even been intimate with each other, but he grabbed me and spoke to me with an intensity I only associate as existing between lovers.

His face falls as he backs away from me and stares at the sad, blank hallway walls. They're psych-ward walls. "Maybe I did, Becka. Maybe I did."

I'm at a complete loss. The level of awkwardness makes me light-headed. I rush out, away, leaving Chase standing alone.

Driving to the store on dimly lit streets, I pray Chase

is simply going through a bizarre, pre-middle age crisis. Perhaps school is stressing him out. It happens. It's happened to other students, and it can happen to him. I focus on avoiding a barrage of potholes in the road while hoping that things get back to normal soon.

I park my Jeep outside the Acme. It's in a bad, high-crime neighborhood, so I walk swiftly toward the store while keeping an eye out for anyone suspicious. I grab a shopping cart and toss in the first premade sandwich I see. It looks horrible, but possibly edible, and I'm too tired to cook tonight. I push the cart aimlessly down the aisles. In the baking goods section, I glance at colorful boxes of cake batter and immediately wish I hadn't. I slam my eyes shut, but it's too late. The cake mixes trigger something awful in me, the snarling, almost lecherous craving that comes as mindlessly as an instinct. I don't bother fighting it.

I storm down one aisle after another and throw in five packages of ramen noodles and two containers of cookie dough. I'm on a rampage, a complete maniac recklessly swerving a shopping cart throughout the store. I knock down a display of crackers and leave them lying on the floor. I almost hit an old woman scrutinizing jars of jelly but I don't pause. I keep tossing food in my cart without looking at price or type. A gallon of ice cream. A jug of milk

Enough! I get in line to check out. I eye my cart, feel guilty, and look away as the cashier rings me up. This is such a strange purchase, she must know something's wrong with me. I half-hope she'll stop me from buying it, but I know she can't and won't. I throw cash at her, hurry to the Jeep with my stash and speed home.

I only barely notice the potent smell of weed on my way to the apartment. I unlock my door, slowly open it, and peek around for Chase. His bedroom door is closed, so I assume he's in there. I tiptoe inside with my bags and sneak into the living room, then the kitchen. I don't see Chase. I think I'm safe.

I open the bags on the counter and robotically start putting the groceries away. I hold up one container of cookie dough and sigh longingly. I want it so bad, but not now. I shove both cookie doughs and the five packs of ramen noodles in a cabinet below the sink. I open the premade sandwich and take a bite. It's stale and awful. I spit it into the trash can and throw the rest away. I remember that I have some leftover tomato sauce and decide to have spaghetti instead. I find a large metal pot, fill it with water, slam it down on a stove burner and set it to boil.

While it's boiling, I decide to call my parents. I haven't spoken to them in a while and maybe a phone call will help me be strong and keep me from binging. Maybe.

I sit on my bed and wait for my parents to answer. It rings twice, three times. By the fifth ring the machine picks up, so I leave a message. I lean my head against a soft, oversized leopard print pillow and close my eyes for five minutes. Sometimes, forcing myself to sleep makes me forget about my hoard.

My body abruptly jerks awake. I've slept longer than five minutes, and I panic. I've left the water boiling! I fly through the door and into the kitchen.

Chase, in a t-shirt and boxer shorts, is standing at the kitchen table with his back to me. One of his legs is propped up on a chair. He has a large hypodermic needle in his right hand and sticks it in his leg. I silently cringe the moment he breaks skin. He lifts his leg violently off the chair, it topples over and hits the floor with a thud. Chase spins and glares at me.

"Were you watching me?" Chase asks through gritted teeth.

"What? No..." I whisper. "I was...boiling a pot of water." My stomach feels like a butterfly cage. I left my phone in my bedroom and he looks rabid.

"Did you see me giving myself a shot?" He peers at me suspiciously.

My instincts say I shouldn't lie to a man who just stabbed himself in the leg. "Yeah, I did," I answer, trying to sound nonchalant. "So what was that?"

"Vitamin B12. I have to give myself a Vitamin B12 shot. My blood is borderline anemic."

"Oh." I nod as if everything makes sense now. I hope he

doesn't sense my doubt. He never told me he was anemic. I'm pretty sure one has to go to the doctor's office to receive a B12 shot, but maybe not. Maybe there's a do-it-yourself kit. He's still staring at me and I mentally beg him to stop. Suddenly, as if he hears my telepathic plea, he stalks past me and down the hall. I hear his bedroom door slam shut

The nerves in my gut feel like machine guns firing in infinite directions and my head might explode like a bomb. I inhale and exhale deeply, and turn off the boiling pot. Most of the water has evaporated. I start crying. I can't even boil water.

I throw open the cupboard doors and desperately search for a large bowl. Finding one, I slam it on the counter and grab a spoon from the drawer. My hands are shaking violently. I kneel on the floor and retrieve the ramen and cookie dough from my stash in the bottom cabinet. I seize a bottle of canola oil and pour some in the bowl. I tear open all five packages of noodles and break off pieces of raw ramen, dip them in the oil and shove them in my mouth. After a few bites the dry noodles are scratching my throat so I snag the gallon of milk from the refrigerator and drink straight from the bottle. Now I'm alternating back and forth between eating hunks of uncooked ramen and canola oil, and slugging milk from the container.

The cookie dough beckons me next. I tear one open and dump it in a separate bowl, along with more milk and oil. I roughly stir the contents and start shoveling the mixture down my gullet.

I think about Chase. I think about school and medicine and about Matthew dumping me. I gorge myself manically, as if this spoonful is Chase, this one is Matthew, and this one, tests and stress and disgusting anatomical facts. I chug more milk. My mid-section feels like it might burst open and slosh onto the kitchen floor. I run to the bathroom and turn on the shower so Chase can't hear me gagging. I fall to my knees in front of the toilet, and stick my finger down my throat.

The food comes up easily in slimy globs, splashing down into the water and dousing my face. Disgusted, I wipe it off with the back of my hand and pick the bile bits from my hair. And then I vomit again. Rinse, and repeat.

With each finger-triggered upheaval, I feel release. I'm ridding myself of everything and everyone. It's not just half-digested food. It's never just that. It's always so much more. Tonight it's Chase, and it's Matthew. And it's loneliness, and heartbreak. I can never seem to shake these things, but I can flush them away.

6

The grounds surrounding the Lenlock Center, a world-renowned eating disorder clinic, are an inviting emerald green. The clean white building with its wraparound front porch looks more like a country inn than a rehabilitation center. I park my Jeep and think back to the last time I was here, that time as a visitor. I had come with my friend Eric to see an old college friend of his, Jana. She was bored and wanted something to read. Ironically, perhaps cruelly, he brought her a book titled Skinny Legs and All.

She welcomed us on the porch, all five feet, four inches, and eighty-seven pounds of her. Her skin was dry and flaky with a sickly yellow tint. When she noticed I was chewing gum, her green eyes bulged and her skeletal hands came down on my shoulders. She begged for a stick, and even though gum was prohibited at the clinic, I pitied her and gave her a piece. We followed her over to a tiny garden. She knelt down, dug a hole in the moist soil and buried the gum, like a dog with a prized bone. Even though I was and had been struggling with bulimia for a time, I swore then and there I'd never get bad enough to have to come to Lenlock.

Months later, I find myself walking down a narrow gravel path and up those same porch steps. They don't seem so welcoming now. I'm sweating in black jogging pants and a pink sweatshirt. An obese white woman is on the porch swing, talking to visitors. She looks at me and smiles. I smile back, wondering how the swing hasn't broken by now. She's obviously an overeater. To my right I see pale, stick-thin girls chatting away. Collectively, they look like a box of matches. The anorexics. Bulimics usually look normal, or even slightly overweight. I don't see any as I enter the clinic. Maybe they're somewhere puking.

The claustrophobic waiting room is mostly empty. I sit down with a magazine from a scattered pile but before I can start reading it, a tall, slim middle-aged woman opens a side door and calls my name.

"Becka?" she inquires amiably. She's wearing a sleek black dress, professional but also sexy, with a pair of purple high heels. Her jet black hair is shiny and cut in a trendy style and she's wearing a lot of makeup. I think she's attractive, though I'd never call her beautiful. What strikes me most are three prominent, horizontal wrinkles on her forehead. They are so well defined and deep that they remind me of crevices between flat, peach-colored rocks. I make a mental note to be polite and not stare at them during my session.

"Hi," I reply, jumping to my feet. "Nice to meet you."

"Likewise, Becka." She cheerfully shakes my hand. "I'm Jessica, your counselor. I know we spoke on the phone a few times, but it's great to meet you in person. Please, follow me to my office."

Jessica's office is at the end of the hall. Her space consists of a cluttered desk, a red chair, framed photos of smiling faces, a brown leather loveseat and two fancy diplomas on the wall. I plop down on the loveseat as she daintily lowers herself into the red chair.

"Well, welcome to Lenlock, Becka! I know this is your first time and you're probably a little nervous, but I promise I don't bite." Her smile is genuine and reassuring. "This is your initial intake, and what that means is I'll ask you some questions to get a better idea of who you are and then have you fill out a few forms. Your answers will help me tailor a therapeutic regime just for you. Please don't feel like you absolutely must answer all my questions. There are no wrong answers. Just relax and tell me what you can. Okay?"

I nod. It doesn't sound awful. Her questions can't kill me.

"Alright then. Why don't you start by telling me how long you've been bulimic?" Everything about Jessica seems sincere, so I decide to be open and up-front.

"Well, I started when I was seventeen, my senior year in high school. I'm twenty-five now, so I guess about seven years."

Her eyes widen ever-so slightly. "That's a fairly long time. And, if I recall correctly from our phone conversation, you were valedictorian of your high school class and recruited to play soccer at a military college? That must have been rigorous! Also..." she checks her notes. "You got a scholarship for medical school? Wow, Becka, that's truly impressive given your bulimia. Truly." She looks back up at me, eyes imploring. "Do you remember why you started throwing up?"

"Not exactly. The memory is cloudy now. I was an avid soccer player and remember thinking that if I lost weight, I'd be a faster runner. I started counting calories and restricting my diet. Then one day after lunch at school, I went to the bathroom, locked myself in a stall, stuck my finger down my throat and made myself vomit. It was a total rush. Really, it felt like an accomplishment. After that I remember showing my best friend how to do it. She's, uh...she's still bulimic." I regret teaching Amy, one of my childhood best friends and soccer teammates, how to properly purge. At first, she couldn't believe it. You could eat whatever you wanted and then throw it up so you wouldn't gain a pound? It sounded immaculate to her. Eight years later she was still tiredly battling bulimia and trying to gain control of her life.

Jessica interrupts my reverie and turns back to her notes. "Do you only binge and purge? Any excessive exercising or laxative use?"

I shudder in response. "Yes and yes."

"How many times a day do you vomit?"

"When it got really bad, my senior year in college, I was binging and purging about seven times a day. Now, it's not that bad. Maybe once a day. It just bothers me, because it makes me so exhausted and then I don't want to do anything. I've been denying it for a long time now, like tellin' myself it's not a real problem, so that's why I forced myself to come here. I'm tired of lettin' it eat up my life."

"I completely understand that feeling," Jessica agrees thoughtfully, not acknowledging my accidental pun. "Tell me, what's your relationship like with your dad?"

Here we go. Of course, she would ask that. Every shrink, therapist and psychologist asks about your relationship with your parents. "It's fine," I answer.

"How about with your mother?"

"It's okay. She can be intense at times, but other than that, it's fine. I had to study a lot as a kid, get good grades and just work a lot. When I got good grades, life was good. If, say, I got a bad grade, like a B, she wasn't thrilled, but I guess that's like all parents."

"How do you mean, intense?" Jessica asks.

I think for a moment. I can't think of any other words for her. "It's… well…" I stumble, searching. "I mean, she's just intense. She has an agenda for you and that's that."

"An agenda. For you? So what would happen if you

deviated from that agenda?"

I hesitate. "She'd get upset. We'd fight. Might not talk to me for a while. That sort of thing."

"Hmm, so your relationship sounds tumultuous? Maybe a bit strained? It sounds like there's no real boundaries set between the two of you."

I want to roll my eyes at Jessica for so ineptly trying to use the power of suggestion. She might as well read my palm while I'm here. By this time, I've seen a good number of therapists and psychiatrists, and I notice a trend. They all try to villainize your parents. Maybe my parents were tough when it came to getting good grades, but I was a bold, impulsive kid. If it wasn't for their strictness, I might have dropped out of school in eighth grade when I started to realize the stifling uselessness of formal education. And who doesn't have at least one thing messed up during childhood? Is there even such a thing as a normal childhood? I don't want to blame my childhood or my parents. I just want to be fixed.

"I think it was exactly as strained as any other mother-daughter relationship. Most mother-daughter relationships are tumultuous," I calmly respond.

She nods but looks dissatisfied. Her expression betrays that she already knows the root of my problem and wants me to provide her with supporting evidence. I don't think she's going to change what she's decided, even if our conversations don't support her theory. I sigh. She's one of those people who goes by the books. The medical rule books, that is. The books are the rules that shrinks and therapists follow, full of guidance and expert opinions, the Bibles quoted by professionals when their judgment is questioned. Deviating from the books is too risky, both emotionally and legally, too intimate, and too involved. No one has the time or the energy to deviate from the books, and no one wants to get sued. It's tough to get sued if you follow the rule books exactly.

The problem is, I don't feel like my mind fits an exact diagnosis. My mind, like everyone's mind, is a mysterious, vast world that's barely been explored. How could it fit under one confining category? Whenever I see a shrink or a therapist, it seems as if they purposefully tweak and manipulate my mind till it does fit, or until I believe the label I'm given. The goal is a nice clean classification, and since I despise labels, I despise the books.

Again, Jessica interrupts my internal monologue and asks me a few more questions. I stay pleasant and answer as best I can. She hands me a few forms to fill out, mostly surveys, and excuses herself. She is back in a few minutes and hands me a script along with a sample of pills.

"I want you to try these," she says, handing them to me. A psychiatrist, who oversees the Eating Disorder clinic, has prescribed them. I haven't met him and probably never will. The drugs are given to me almost like protocol.

"The side effects are listed on the paper inside the sample and you'll get more when you fill the script. But let me know if anything unusual happens. You may get a dry mouth from the pills so drink lots of water."

She didn't mention the antidepressant would completely muzzle my emotions and could turn my world upside down. But I dutifully schedule my next appointment and exchange amicable goodbyes.

On my drive home, I stop at a local high school track. I think I might run a few miles to clear my head, hopefully recharge so I can study for my Boards. I'm taking them in a week, but for now I don't want to think. I want to run. Running gives me that brief, wonderful moment where my mind is uncluttered and free.

I'm cooled down after walking back to my car. I feel lighter, energetic. I check my phone. One message—from Chase.

"Something's come up. You need to get home, now."

7

The scenery on the way home is a blur. I'm praying that nothing serious is wrong. What if something happened to Moses? Lately she's been resting on Chase's bedroom window sill, and he leaves the window open half the time. I don't know what I'd do if I lost that cat. Right now, she's my only link to normalcy.

The elevator opens. I sprint to my apartment door, unlock it and lunge inside.

"Moses?" I yell as I sweep the apartment with my eyes. "Moses! Come here!" I hear her token meow. She runs out from behind the living room couch and rubs up against my legs, mewing for attention. I kneel, rub her head and give her a kiss.

"Chase?" I call from the living room. "Are you home?"

No answer. It's Saturday so maybe he's out running errands. I temporarily forget his earlier message and the urgency in his voice, and decide to make a peanut butter and jelly sandwich when the front door slams.

"Chase?" I shout, "I'm in the kitchen!"

Chase, wearing a ripped blue t-shirt and khaki shorts, steps into the kitchen and stares at me. He looks frazzled. His brown eyes are blazing. I feel a familiar sinking sensation.

"Becka," Chase starts in a grave, monotone voice, "where did you get the television in the living room?" He steps closer to me. "Did you put a camera inside the TV, Becka? Did you?!"

I retreat and lean against the counter. I'm cornered. I try to remember where the big, bulky TV set on our living room floor originated.

"My dad. My dad bought it for me. I think he got it from...Circuit City?" I offer.

Chase grimaces and screams. "Don't lie to me, Becka! Do not lie to me! I have a magazine that lists every model of televisions that can have security cameras installed, and that TV is one of them. I checked last night. Don't lie, I can always tell when you're lying."

Shocked, I drop my peanut butter and jelly sandwich on the floor. He's got to be joking, and a very anxious laugh escapes my lips. This isn't real.

"Chase, are you serious? What is wrong with you? I just told you, my dad bought me that TV at Circuit City. You think I installed a camera in there? To do what, film you? You... you don't even leave your bedroom! Why would I want to film you? I don't even have a tool box! I wouldn't know how…" I started off shouting, but my voice drifts off.

I feel crazy justifying why I wouldn't and couldn't install a camera in a TV. His accusation is so absurd that I figure he must be kidding. That must be it. Except for his face which is serious and threatening. I don't like it; he looks tormented. I want him to calm down so I can move out of this corner, away from him and his crazy face.

"I have proof!" he angrily exclaims. His warm spit splatters my cheek. He runs down the hall, only to return seconds later with his laptop.

"Look!" he screams, stabbing his finger at his computer screen. "Look! I know you've been on my computer! I can prove it! Why, though? Why would you do this to me? Why are you, of all people, trying to sabotage me? Do you think I'm in the Mafia or something?"

I'm rendered speechless. All I can do is shake my head side to side. Chase huffs, kicks his right leg in the air, turns furiously and storms down the hall. I hear his door nearly come off its hinges as he jerks it open and slams it closed.

Once I catch my breath, I hurriedly gather up my things, bolt out of the apartment and drive to the library. I need to get somewhere normal, fast. I run a stop sign and hope no cops see me. I screech into the school parking lot and hurry inside. I claim a cubicle and begin studying for my Boards.

Considering my shaky state of mind, I'm actually quite productive. My eyes are glued to the material and my mind is in sponge-mode, absorbing knowledge effortlessly. It's a feeling I haven't experienced in a long time.

Hours pass and the sun sets. I'm afraid to go home, so I decide to sleep in the library.

Monday comes too quickly. My alarm didn't go off, so I'm running late. I throw on a shirt over a pair of jeans and rush to school for my morning class. I glance around the main lecture hall. Chase, as usual, isn't there. I'm not sure if I'm worried or relieved.

When the lecture ends, I head to the cafeteria for a much needed coffee. In the hall I see Matthew chatting to a first year, Stacey. My heart drops as I quickly look away. Stacey? Really? Not only is she unattractive with her nest of Raggedy Ann hair and fifty unnecessary pounds, but she's also a total bitch. I walk past them and pretend I don't care.

"Becka!" a gruff male voice calls my name. "Becka, I'd like to talk to you for a minute."

I turn around and see one of my professors, Dr. H, smiling at me. I return the gesture and agree to follow him to his office.

He sits behind his desk as I sit in front. His drooping grey mustache combined with his plump figure makes him look like a talking walrus. "Sorry to pull you out of your day like this, but Chase came to my office this morning. He had his laptop with him and said people were tampering with his computer. He, well...he mentioned your name as one of those people."

His words shock me like a cattle prod. I have no rebuttal. Never did I think Chase would take his accusations this far, to involve the faculty. He's completely out of line. He took his crazy antics too far this time. I can feel my body temperature rise by the second.

"Dr. H, I've never used Chase's computer," I snap.

The walrus clears his throat and wiggles in his seat.

"I'm not accusing you of anything here, Becka. Please know that. Chase tried to show me on his computer how he knows people are tampering with his notes, emails, bank accounts and such. Claimed they are sabotaging his medical career. None of it made any sense to me, trust me on that. I know he went to the Dean's office, too. Told him the same thing he told me."

"He's been acting extremely strange lately. Maybe he needs to talk to someone, did you suggest that?" I ask cautiously. I'm not sure whose side the doctor is on.

"No. No, I didn't suggest that. He also alleges that you might have put a camera of some sort in a television set? I realize this sounds insane, but he insisted that you were filming him while you weren't home. I mean, he was awfully upset about it."

My head feels like it's going to explode from shock, anger, and pure absurdity. I want to hit Chase and smack

Dr. H for even asking me such a question. At the same time, I want to fall off the chair laughing. This is how a person is driven crazy, I think, before answering Dr. H.

"Dr. H," I start, trying to contain my contempt, "I have no idea how to put a video camera in a TV. Nor do I have any desire to film Chase. And this is completely stupid to add, but my TV is in our living room. Chase never leaves his bedroom. If my intent was to film him while I'm not home, why the heck would I put a camera in the living room TV? To film dust gathering?"

Once again, I think I'm coming across like a lunatic trying too hard to prove I'm not insane. I warn myself to shut up. The more I say the crazier I feel, and the crazier I'm sure I sound.

Dr. H continues arguing, but I tune out the walrus. Instead, I'm internally debating how best to handle my situation with Chase. On one hand, I want to confront him and fight it out. But that would take energy I don't have, and I fear my classwork would suffer. Plus, I don't think I'd win. I have a hunch he's too far gone. I briefly consider moving out, but again, I have to study and moving is a huge hassle I don't need. I tell myself that my goal is to get through school as painlessly and successfully as possible, and to do that, I have to avoid Chase as much as possible. In a roomful of two people, I have to be invisible.

8

It's Wednesday afternoon. Friday is my last final in med school, and instead of studying, I'm sitting in Dr. Jonas' office. It's my second time here. The first time was months ago, and I'm fairly certain she was shocked I called for another appointment.

Dr. Jonas is a psychologist. She's petite with short grey hair, wears thin glasses, and dresses like a nun. I heard about her through a friend who told me she's not only good, but sees students at a discounted rate. I'm like a desperate whore these days when it comes to therapists. I'm willing to give anyone a go.

She's currently on the phone. While I wait across the desk from her, I glance around her peculiar office. It's actually a spare room in her house, and that makes me uncomfortable. The walls and floor are a pale pink. Numerous old-fashioned dolls in Victorian dresses and several pastel-colored doll castles are scattered throughout the room. It reminds me of a five year-old girl's playroom. I hate dolls. They're creepy, plastic, miniature humans who probably come alive at night and kill people.

"I'm so sorry, Becka," Dr. Jonas apologizes, hanging up the phone. "That was my son. He has a big soccer game tonight and was giving me directions. You played soccer too, right?"

I nod, wondering where this is leading.

"That's great. It's such a wonderful game to watch. So, where were we? Ah, yes! The book I lent you the first time you were here. Did you read it?" Dr. Jonas looks at me expectantly.

I nod again. The book she assigned me was called The Borderline Mother. I remember driving home from my first session and skimming the pages. I never read it in its entirety. It described characters with borderline personality traits, particularly mothers. The book implied that Alice's mother in Alice in Wonderland was plagued with borderline personality disorder. Interesting analogy, but I had no idea what that had to do with me.

So I asked. "Yes, I read it. How is that supposed to relate to my situation, exactly?"

"I'm glad you asked! Were you able to see how the Queen and the Duchess' cook are all different characterizations of Alice's overbearing mother? And how those might appear as projections of a borderline personality?"

Again, that expectant look, but I'm at a loss. I don't

remember the Queen of Hearts slashing her forearms or threatening suicide, two common traits of Borderlines. In fact, she's more into chopping off other people's heads. The Duchess' cook, the way she throws dishes and pepper around, reminds me of someone with anger management issues. Maybe she was sick of her job and cracked. Maybe they're pre-menopausal and dealing with hormonal fluctuations.

"Um, I don't really see that...but maybe?" I shrug, completely unsure of myself. I know better than to straight-up disagree with a shrink. It's a lot easier to agree during the session and disagree once you're gone.

"Becka, I think you might exhibit borderline traits," Dr. Jonas intones with deep sincerity. "I'll need more time, of course, but that's my initial assessment. And that could be why you have trouble forming long, lasting relationships."

I cringe and look away when she slaps that label on me. I was just dumped by my boyfriend, one more strike in the relationship game. He probably thinks I'm a borderline psycho. Or a psycho borderline. That's why he dumped me. I feel my eyes welling with tears.

"I don't know. I've never heard that before," I mutter, staring at my knees.

"Oh, well, sometimes these things run in families. Maybe your mother? Your grandmother?"

"Ambiguity runs in my family."

She looks peeved. "Becka, often Borderlines become

that way because they had a significant figure in their life who was borderline, and that's the only way they know how to interact with other people. But it doesn't mean you're a lost cause. With medication and therapy, these things are treatable." She delivers this prognosis calmly, staring at me the whole time.

The label doesn't feel right to me, like an ill-fitting jacket. She's the expert, so there's no convincing her, but it can't be right. I squirm in my chair. I want to tell her every single person on earth exhibits some traits of mental disorder, but I don't want to start a fight. It's not like she'd believe me. She's the doctor and I'm the patient, even though seeing patients among an army of dolls hints of her own mental issues. I look up, straight into the eyes of a beautiful doll with long locks of golden curls. I want to smash its porcelain face.

"Okay. So are you saying I'm only borderline borderline?" I ask, thinking the sooner I agree with her, the sooner I can leave and never talk to her again.

She scowls at me. She must think I'm mocking her initial analysis by being silly, or pretending to not understand. But I'm not pretending; I have no idea where she came up with this assessment. She reaches over to her desk, picks up a diagnostic manual, and reads a passage on borderline personality disorder. Like an obedient dog, I sit and listen. I'm still listening when she proceeds to paraphrase what she just read, rehashing the same information in slightly different words, but none of it makes any sense. I can't make that label fit. It's like trying to make a relationship work with the wrong person.

Her phone rings, and I use that as my cue. "You know, Dr. Jonas, thank you so much for seeing me today, but I really have to run. I have a huge exam in two days. Feel free to answer your phone. I'll...call?" I babble and jump out of my seat.

"Oh! Are you sure? I wanted to discuss medications. Well, if you must, of course...Good luck on your test! I'm sure you'll do fine. Focus. And please, do call. Interruptions to your therapy will not get you better," she says while picking up the phone.

I wave and walk away.

On the drive home I refuse to think of shrinks and labels, ill-fitting jackets, or the Queen of Hearts. It'll only make me angry. It might make me crash. I blast the oldies station, roll down my window, and let the warm spring wind massage my face.

9

I set up a study area at my kitchen table and set some coffee to brew, then head to my room. I'm going to be up all night studying, so I might as well change into my pajamas.

As I'm passing Chase's room, he opens his door. I avert my eyes, duck into my room, and close the door. Ever since my meeting with Dr. H, I've been tiptoeing around Chase. He seems to be ignoring me as well. Whenever we pass each other in the hallway, we acknowledge one another with a nod and keep walking, like strangers on the street.

Sometimes, despite myself, I'll hesitate, hoping he'll notice and either crack a joke or suggest getting a bite to eat. It's always silence instead. He's lost about twenty pounds and looks like a cancer victim in torn, stained clothes that haven't been washed in days. His hair sticks up in myriad directions and there's a look of desperate hunger in his eyes, like a vicious, starving animal. Something is very wrong, but I can't pinpoint it.

It's two in the morning and pitch black out. I'm sleep-deprived, practically delirious, yet still slumped at the kitchen table studying when the apartment door crashes shut.

"Chase?" I call apprehensively.

No answer. I stare into the dark living room and see a shadow coming toward me.

He answers quietly. "Yes. It's me. I went out to get some food."

I'm surprised he made a food run. He hasn't left the apartment in so long. Maybe it's a sign he's getting better.

He places a grocery bag on the kitchen table. I look up from my studies, smile at him, then glance back down at my books. A minute passes. I'm hoping he's preparing food, but no, he's still standing there. I glance at him again, uneasily. He's staring at me. My synapses tick like a time bomb.

"Becka, do you remember when I went to get my hair cut a couple of days ago?" Chase asks, watching my reaction closely.

I don't remember. His hair doesn't look that much different to me, so I wonder if he even got it cut. "No, Chase. I don't. But I might have been out." I make a show of diving back into my books, hoping he'll take that as a sign to leave me alone. No such luck.

"Oh. Maybe you were. I drove to Connecticut to get my hair cut. Do you know why the dean would follow me there? He followed me in his car all the way from

Philadelphia to Connecticut."

I sigh. The last thing I need is an interrogation session with Chase right before a monumental exam that could make or break my grade point average. I highly doubt the dean followed him. That's insane, though insanity seems to be the norm lately. I want this to end. "No, Chase, I don't."

"Well, he did. Did you say anything to him? Do you think I'm in the Mafia?"

Beads of sweat gather on my forehead. My breath quickens. This is absurd. No, this is psychotic. How long will this joke go on? "Chase, this is insane. NO. No, I don't think you're in the Mafia and no, I didn't tell the dean a damn thing about you!"

"Then why did you bug the apartment, Becka? Why are you doing this to me?"

"What?! What the fuck are you talking about, Chase? I didn't bug shit! I have no…"

Chase interrupts my tirade by pounding the wall with the palm of his hand and screaming.

"Do not talk to me in here! We can no longer talk here, it's bugged. I refuse to speak to you in this apartment anymore. If you want to talk to me, it'll have to be outside in the garden."

My body tingles, then starts vibrating all over. I can no longer ignore the strangling tension felt in every corner of our apartment. I know I'm going to snap, and this time I can't stop it.

I pick up a dish and slam it against the wall. I watch as it shatters to pieces while the sound of broken glass delights my ears. I smash a glass against the floor. Then another one, and another. I am the Duchess' cook.

The kitchen floor is covered with shards. I can't see straight through the rage. My head is spinning, or it might be the room. I pick up a book and hurl it, hard, squarely into Chase's malnourished chest.

"Stop it!" I scream through a flood of tears as I collapse in a heap among the sharp broken bits. I pull my knees into my chest and weep. "Why are you doing this to me? Why the hell are you doing this to me? Stop it, please, for the love of Christ, get away from me! Leave me alone, Chase, please, just leave me the hell alone!"

Chase stands still, completely dumbfounded, like a puppy that doesn't understand why it's being scolded. He slowly pushes a piece of broken glass across the kitchen floor with his bare foot, turns around, and locks himself in his bedroom where he stays the rest of the night.

I sit on the floor crying for another ten minutes. I pull myself halfway together and sweep up the glass. I crawl back into the kitchen chair and stare blankly at my books.

I can't focus on studying. All I can see is the mess of boxes and dirty clothes on Chase's floor, the weight he's lost, the extra pack per day of cigarettes he's smoking. Even though I'm exhausted, physically and emotionally, I wish I could bust down his door, dress him, and drag him to a diner. I'd force food down his throat if I had to. Maybe I can slap it out of him. This is too damn much. Watching him fall victim to an impenetrable bubble of madness is making ME mad.

I leave the books behind and go to my room. I cry, as if Chase recently died and isn't brooding in the room next door. I almost wish he'd die. Seeing him lose his mind feels more painful. At least if he died, I wouldn't have to be teased by seeing his physical body, because the Chase I adore doesn't exist anymore. His body is a house that is falling apart, and his mind is a prisoner in the upstairs attic. I have no hope. Still, sometimes, a glimpse of his malnourished body makes me want to violently shake him until the chains holding his mind captive fall free. As if that would work.

10

It's Thursday, early evening, and my final is tomorrow. My Boards are in two weeks, which means I need to study like a maniac. I'm in the library, again, surrounded by big brains conquering the pathology of diseases. I inhale deeply. It smells like home-cooked leftovers, Taco Bell, coffee and body odor. I doubt some students stop studying to shower.

I'm struggling to memorize every liver disease known to man. An hour passes, then another, and I can't seem to remember anything. My head feels full and stubborn. It can't take much more. Death, death, death in every entry. Life is temporary, I get it. Why is this so painful for me and not for everyone else? I'm even taking an antidepressant. Maybe they're sociopaths? The material is depressing. I want to slam my book shut and go for a run. And then to a bar.

I try to motivate myself. Stop it, Becka, I scold. You have to study. You're too damn sensitive. Don't think about what you're studying, just learn it. If you fail, what else are you going to do? Mop floors? Hand out fries?

I can't stop thinking about the impermanent nature of life. I shouldn't be trapped inside a cubicle fifteen hours a day. I need to leave. I need to do something permanent.

By now it's nine o'clock on a very dark night. I'm in my Jeep, lost, and ready to fight everything that is temporary. And just like in the movies, when you think the heroine is about to go over a cliff, I see it—Cadillac Tattoo.

A rugged-looking woman mans the counter at the parlor. She's wearing a wife-beater, camouflage pants, and her brown hair's slicked back in a neat ponytail. Her dark blue eyes mean business and her playfully inked arms look like a child's picture book.

"I'm Tory, one of the artists here. What can I do for you?" she asks in a no-nonsense manner.

"Well...I have this idea for a tattoo, with music notes and tiger lilies? For my lower back. How much will it be and how long will it take?" I'm nervous. I don't know what I'm getting into. Maybe I should run back to the car. Tattoos are really permanent.

"Sometimes it's best to just draw these things out." Tory grabs a piece of white paper and picks up a pencil. While she silently sketches, I examine the display of tattoos inside the glass counter. Some are cheesy, some are tribal and trendy, the sort that young girls put on their backs to snare attention.

"How's this?" Tory finally asks, holding up the paper. It's

a curving ribbon of musical notes bordered by a tiger lily on either side. I think I like it, except I have no way of telling what it will look like on my back.

"Perfect," I respond. "How much?"

"Three-fifty."

I decide quickly. "Okay. Okay, I'm ready. Will you be doing it?"

"Yep. You want to do the whole thing tonight?"

"Yes. I can't come back. I mean, I can, but knowing me, I probably won't."

Tory doesn't comment on my confusing reply. Instead, she motions me to follow her to the back room. I instantly like her. She's tough but cute, and all business.

She stands behind me and tells me to lean forward. I can feel her pushing up my t-shirt and lowering the band on my jogging pants. Suddenly I wince as a whirring needle hits the tender skin of my lower back. I grip the sides of a table directly in front of me.

Tory continues to work while I mentally command my body to adjust to the pain and discomfort. The needle spills color under my skin. Tory doesn't say a word. I break out in chills. My pain tolerance is high, but each time the needle hits, I feel a new, excruciating sting. It hurts but part of me loves it. All I can think about is the growling device marking my back, and not the morbid sentences in my pathology book. The physicality is a relief.

An hour and a half goes by. I'm still bent over. Heavily pierced and tattooed men have been in and out of the back room, checking out my progress. I feel dirty, a little obscene, and very alive.

I get light-headed all of a sudden. My fingers tingle. I shift my feet forward, and Tory notices.

"Hey, do you want to finish the rest another day?" Her voice comes from over my shoulder.

"No, I'm okay. Keep going." I'm not ready to go back to the library. I want this finished.

"Tell you what. I need a five-minute break. I'm going to buy you a juice. Drink that, and we'll start again."

I nod and take time to stretch while Tory runs to the mini-mart across the street. As promised, she's back in five minutes and hands me an orange juice. I drink it, take a few deep breaths, and then resume my position as a bent-over, living canvas.

Tory fires up the gun again. It still hurts, but less so with some sugar in my bloodstream. Another hour later and she's finally done. She holds up a mirror for me to see the finished product.

"Wow! It's huge!" I exclaim. Part of it drops lower than my lower back. I shrug. Nothing I can do about it now.

"Do you like it?" Tory beams.

The shockingly bright orange flowers, the dancing, lyrical notes. My skin is a poem. "I do!" I answer enthusiastically.

"Can I take a picture of it and hang it up in the parlor?"

I guess I don't mind my lower back on display. "Yeah, sure!"

I thank her, hand her $350 from the conveniently located ATM machine in the parlor, and figure it's not too late to get back to the library and claim an empty cubicle.

And so I sit, studying, almost dozing off, when like lightening the fear of failure strikes bright and fast. I am running out of time. Fear has always motivated me when I needed it most. It keeps me alert and studying until one o'clock Friday morning, the day of my final. I drive home from the library, rush inside my bedroom, barricade the door, and fall into a weary, endorphin-filled oblivion, a routine I will continue for the next two weeks.

11

It's Monday afternoon, a week after my Boards and three weeks after my final, and I'm sitting in Dr. Patel's office at Redeemer Hospital in West Philadelphia. Dr. Patel is a psychiatrist. I'm not a patient, though I probably could be. I'm assigned to this location to complete my required psychiatry clinical rotation. I just got back from visiting my parents who live about two hours outside of the city. I didn't do much, but it was nice to relax, sleep, run and not have to worry about a crazy roommate. I also feel stronger and more upbeat, possibly because my mom cooked good, healthy meals for me, and I kept them down. My parents were always around, like watchmen, and I never binge and purge in front of people. It's disgusting, gross, shameful and something you do alone.

Dr. Patel is a lanky, dark-skinned Indian man with a shiny, greasy mustache and matching black hair. He looks very doctor-like in a tweed suit coat, matching tie and polished shoes that ooze wealth. So far today, we've made morning rounds on patients in the hospital ward and now we're seeing outpatients.

This morning the ward was, well, insane. A complete chorus of crazy. Patients in filthy, torn street clothes or flimsy blue hospital gowns paced up and down the ward, like caged zoo tigers that instinctively know they don't belong there. A twenty-something emaciated psychotic with gnarled dreadlocks and flaming brown eyes yelled at me for ruining his brain. I never saw him before in my life, but he managed to make me look down at my feet and feel guilty. Other patients were arguing over whose turn it was to use the lone payphone connecting them to the outside world.

There was a dreadful dead-fish stench that nearly incapacitated me and made me reach for my rescue inhaler. A nurse noticed and whispered that it came from "Miss Z," a sixty year-old schizophrenic patient with a vicious urinary tract infection, who refused both treatment and showers. I tried to hold my breath and move forward down the hall, but all I could think about was walking through her decaying, bacteria-saturated vaginal cavity. The only thing that kept me moving was fear—fear of the enraged Twenty-Something or someone else attacking me. The potential scenarios played out in my head like a horror movie, and I couldn't hit the Stop button.

Dr. Patel's door whips open, interrupting my thoughts. A thin black boy with a wild Afro stands in the doorway.

His naïve brown eyes nervously scan the room making him look skittish. He's wearing baggy jeans, white sneakers, an oversized white t-shirt and a gold chain. His face is smooth, cute and very young. It must be Jamal, Patel's first patient.

"Is this Dr. Patel's?" he asks with a shaky voice.

I smile, nod and gesture him to take a seat. I tell him Dr. Patel will be back soon. Jamal nods and takes a seat but his legs won't stop shaking. His jittering is contagious. I've already read his chart. His mother brought him to the crisis center a few days ago and claimed that fifteen-year old Jamal talks to himself. She said Jamal closes his bedroom door at night and talks to himself for hours on end. I'm sure Dr. Patel is going to try to rule out schizophrenia.

The door swings open and Dr. Patel walks in. "Hello, Jamal!" He begins in a thick-layered Indian accent. "I'm Dr. Patel. I met your mother the other day, though I think another doctor saw you. I think it was Dr. Khan?"

Jamal furrows his brow. I can tell he can't really understand the doctor. I can barely understand Patel, his accent is that thick. I just purse my lips and nod when he speaks to me. I'm sure his patients do the same thing, which only adds to the ambiguity of diagnosing mental illness.

"Oh! Yeah, yeah," Jamal excitedly exclaims, and slaps his thighs three times. His nervous energy might send him through the roof.

"Okay, then...." Dr. Patel takes a seat in the leather chair behind his desk. "Tell me, Jamal, do you hear voices?"

"Voices? What? No! My momma says I do, but no way. I don't hear voices. I mean, I hear you talking to me but I don't hear no other voices," Jamal insists. His legs are shaking faster now.

"Then why, Jamal, would your mother say that? Your mother told me that you talk to yourself," Dr. Patel presses.

"Talk to myself?" Jamal cries in disbelief. "What? No, no, no. She don't know what she's talking about. I spit. That's what I do."

"You spit? Hmm...But do you hear voices?" Dr. Patel asks. He looks confused.

"Yeah, exactly! I spit it out. I spit out in the mirror sometimes at night. That's what she's talkin' 'bout. I don't hear voices!"

"But your mother, Jamal, has seen you talking to yourself in the mirror. What do the voices say? We have medication that can help you, but you need to tell me what the voices are telling you to do."

I'm in disbelief. The tension between Jamal and Dr. Patel is rising. Their cultures are relentlessly clashing right in front of my eyes, like a sword fight between wealthy India and West Philadelphia. My honest impression of Jamal is that he's bright, sane and doesn't need medication. If anyone sounds crazy, his mother does. Some part of me will not allow me to remain silent. Jamal's young and smart, he has a future.

He doesn't need big-gun medications, and I'm overwhelmed with an urge to save him.

"Dr. Patel," I respectfully say. "When Jamal says he spits in the mirror, it means he's rapping. He's a rapper and that's how he practices."

Dr. Patel stares at me blankly. Nothing registers. I'm a stupid, white girl.

"But he hears voices. Why else would he talk to himself?" Dr. Patel asks.

"No, he spits. He raps. He's not hearing voices. He's practicing to be a musician," I explain.

The conversation continues in this relentlessly circular fashion. Nothing is sinking in. I give up and excuse myself to the bathroom. Let the "expert" seal the young man's fate.

When I come back to Patel's office, Jamal is already gone. I'm relieved. I would have hated to see Patel hand him a prescription for anti-psychotics he doesn't need. I sit back down in my chair while Patel writes a note in Jamal's chart. I remind myself that I need to act interested and engaged so I can get a decent evaluation at the end of this clinical. I ask a question so I'll look motivated.

"Dr. Patel," I say, clearing my throat. "I was wondering, how come patients who hear voices only hear bad voices? Why don't the voices ever say anything good?"

Dr. Patel stares at the wall behind me. His gaze moves up and to the right as he taps his pen against the desk.

"Well… I think it's based on your culture. A person might hear the voice of God in any country if he's very religious. But, say, here in the U.S., one might hear the voice of the bush. And the voice of the bush will tell him to do all sorts of things. In other country, they'll hear another leader."

I have no idea what the man's talking about. The voice of the bush? A talking shrub? Isn't that in the Bible somewhere? "The voice of the bush?"

"Yes. The president. President Bush."

"Oh!" I chuckle. "I was confused for a minute. Okay, that makes sense." I've never heard President Bush called "the bush" until now. First time for everything, I guess.

As lunch time approaches, Dr. Patel tells me to get lunch then visit a few patients we saw together in the morning. He would be gone the rest of the afternoon. I nod in agreement and leave. I decide to skip out on visiting patients, since Patel will never know, and go straight home.

When the elevator opens on my floor, I step out and immediately know something's off. My apartment door is wide open and a man dressed in work clothes is fiddling with the lock.

"Excuse me," I say as I get closer, "What are you doing?"

"Putting in new locks," he says while wiping sweat away from his brow. "Who are you?"

"I live here!" I snap. I scoot past him and yell for Chase inside the apartment. Chase, looking disheveled as usual, pokes his head out of his bedroom door.

"Chase, what is going on? Why are we getting new locks?"

"Because someone has been tampering with my stuff. I needed to change all of the locks and all of my passwords," he says with conviction.

"Jesus. Are you serious? Well, I need a new key now!"

"I have the new keys," Chase says.

"Give me one then, because I want to go to the gym."

"Not yet, Becka. I want to make sure...everything is okay."

"Are you...," I start as anger takes over. I move towards his bedroom, slam my forearm against the door, causing it to open. "Are you fucking kidding me? You need to give me a set of keys, Chase. I am so sick of your twisted mind games. In fact, I don't even know why I go to the ward. I might as well stay home, because THIS is the ward!"

Chase looks calm, much calmer than me. "I will, Becka. I just need to make sure it's okay. Until then...,"

"No! I interrupt while stomping my foot. "I am done with you! If you don't give me a key, I will go straight to management."

"Okay, okay," Chase says with a nervous, gentle laugh. "Geez, you are trigger happy."

"Now!"

Chase hands me a key when I notice Moses sitting in his wide-open window.

"Jesus, Chase!" I scurry over, scoop her up and hold her

close with my left arm while slamming the window shut with my right. "I told you this window can't be open! If she falls, she's dead! She would never survive that fall! I told you!"

"I know, I know, I'm sorry. I would never hurt her. I just forgot. I'm sorry."

"You can't forget! She trusts you and you can't forget!" I yell. Tears are welling up in my eyes. Thinking I may have put Moses in danger by living with a crazy man makes me hate myself. Chase continues to apologize but I tune him out, stroke Moses' fur, head into my room and slam the door shut.

12

Tuesday morning, back on the ward, and I'm fighting to keep my head up. I didn't sleep well, mostly because I thought Chase was going to kill me or Moses. I made sure she was with me in my bedroom all night long, but this morning, after five cups of coffee, I left the apartment tired and with a sick, ominous feeling in my stomach. I told myself that Chase loves Moses, left the window open by mistake, and would never hurt her. That's what I told myself, but I planned on hurrying home as soon as I could.

"Hey, Becka!" I hear as I'm leaning against the nurse's station doing nothing but trying to stay awake. I look up and see Jamal.

"Jamal!" I say. "What are you doing here?"

He's smiling and that's when I notice his adorable dimples. I didn't notice them yesterday, but I didn't see him smile yesterday either. He looks too cute and young to be crazy. It feels wrong to lock up dimples like his.

"My mom brought me back last night," he says, still

beaming. He seems happy, almost too happy, nothing like the nervous Jamal I met yesterday. Maybe they drugged him.

"Oh!" I say while wondering what caused his mom to bring him here. "Are you feeling okay?"

"I'm good, I'm good!"

He positions himself directly in front of my face and starts talking. I listen but have trouble following him. He starts telling me that he's not only a rapper, but a poet and spends most of his time writing poems and that writing is his favorite thing to do. Then he elaborates on a few he's written. I notice his speech is fast, and his ideas go in all sorts of directions, like ants swarming on a sidewalk. I assume he's manic. And if he's manic, he'll talk to me forever, so I acknowledge his dual talent, and politely advise him that I have something urgent to do in the doctors' lounge. He nods his head automatically, but his baby-face eyes look sad and rejected.

"Tell you what. Let me see if I can find some scrap paper so you can write poems or songs," I say.

His face lights up and he enthusiastically nods his head, making his Afro look like a bush being rocked by a tornado.

I grab Jamal's chart first. He was brought to the psychiatric emergency room by his mother who said he was "walking the streets half-naked at 2am and talking nonsense to someone invisible." She also said he might be doing drugs. "Schizophrenia" is listed as a presumptive diagnosis. I shrug, snatch some scrap paper, and head back out into the hallway.

Jamal smiles brightly when he sees me. Not wanting to get dragged into another long-winded, scattered conversation, I hand him the paper and tell him to write. He performs an ecstatic jig which makes me laugh.

Later that afternoon, when I come back to the ward after lunch, Jamal's impatiently pacing up and down the hallway. When he sees me, he waves a paper in the air and scurries over.

"Becka! Becka!" he hollers. "I got something for you!" He's so excited that he nearly knocks me over. With a big grin, he hands me the piece of paper I gave him earlier and says, "A poem. For you!"

I smile back at him. My cheeks feel warm. I wasn't expecting a personal poem. It wasn't my original intention and it feels a bit unprofessional. Still, I'm just happy he's writing and continuing his passion, a healthy one, in the ward. I don't want to discourage him, so I accept the sheet of paper and say, "Thank you! How thoughtful."

I glance over my shoulder and see Dr. Patel watching us with a peculiar look on his face. I duck past Jamal into the doctors' lounge where I can read in peace.

> Days are long / time is short
> Petty Face / will not hit you / so no court
> I love your eyes / as well as your hips
> Look at ya petty/ fine silky lips

I don't know where / to start, but
You can take any pieces of my heart
Please don't leave me in the dark
You remind me of my X / not all about sex
Yeah God is in my life / don't want no wife
But you feel like you know make me right
Take long to hold 'em / easy ta throw'em
Eazy to fall in love / hard to fall out
Let me find out /man got that ring finger
That's cool / I'm an artist/ plus real sing

I fold up the poem and tuck it away in my white coat's side pocket. I don't know whether to laugh or cry. His words are adorable and flattering, yet revealing of the life he leads; a life I will never completely understand no matter how many stories he tells or poems he writes.

I sigh and walk back into the hallway where Dr. Patel is chatting with one of the nurses. He sees me and motions me to follow him to his office. Once there, he sits in his leather chair. I stand behind his desk like a schoolkid about to be scolded by the principal.

"Becka," he says with a critical voice. "I just spoke to Jamal. He told me he wrote you a poem."

"Yes, he did," I reply with relief, having thought Patel was going to yell at me. "I talked to him earlier in the hallway. He told me he was a rapper and a poet, so I gave him some paper to write on."

"I see. Well, you know, you need to be careful. You don't

want to encourage these people. You need to maintain a safe, professional distance," Dr. Patel chides me authoritatively.

"He just wanted something to do," I defend my action, a bit spitefully.

"Oh, I realize that. You just need to be careful. It's easy for these patients to develop crushes on their main caregivers. Sometimes those relationships are the most intimate ones they have in their lives. For example, Jamal just wrote you a poem. A love poem, I'm assuming? So you need to work on maintaining a professional distance."

I nod and look at the wall, hoping he won't ask to see Jamal's poem, because it is kind of a love poem. "His poem is harmless. I just thought it was good for him to write, since the ward is so dry and boring."

I got the last word, the most genuine thing I could say out loud and not get kicked out of the rotation. What I wanted to say was that most of the patients are restlessly meandering, drooling, sleeping, or loitering around the nurses' station all day long. I wanted to comment on how they're hunched over in a lobotomized line for a cupful of pills or a tray of food and look more like bizarre props than people. I wanted to tell him to forget the medication and give them something meaningful to do. But I didn't say any of that.

"There's a new patient. I have his chart here. Look it over," Dr. Patel barks, interrupting my thoughts on Jamal and the pathetic plight of all the patients.

The new patient is Mr. Lions, a thirty-eight year old black male who was arrested the previous night and brought to the hospital for threatening to kill his grandmother with a knife. He has a history of antisocial personality disorder, schizoaffective disorder, random outbursts of violence, sexual assault, and was in prison for two years for manslaughter. I arc an eyebrow.

"If you're finished, why don't you interview him and then present him to me? He's in room 102." He dismisses me with a wave.

At the end of the hallway I timidly knock on the door of room 102. "Mr. Lions?"

No one responds, so I knock again and slowly push open the door and enter the room. I see a thin, muscular man in a white hospital gown lying face down in bed. My instinct is to let sleeping dogs alone, but Patel wants a report.

"Mr. Lions? Sorry to disturb you," I politely squeak.

Mr. Lions still doesn't budge. I watch his chest go up and down and wait for a sign that he might be willing to talk to me. He doesn't look like a murderer. Well, at least not while he's sleeping.

Suddenly his head shoots up and he glares at me. Surprised, I jump backward toward the door. His gaze is detached and emotionless. I've seen that look before in the eyes of my parents' vicious dog Cerberus, right before he lunged at someone. Lions lifts his arm and slaps it hard against his mattress, like a wild bear stomping a paw before attacking. My heart quickens. I step backward again while keeping my eyes on Mr. Lions. I think I might have to fight him and quickly picture kicking him in the groin, grabbing a handful of his crotch, twisting and pulling hard like I'm starting a lawn mower. Scratch that. I decide to run instead. "You know… I'll just come back," I stammer as I turn on my heels and zip out the door.

Back in Zombie Land after lunch, the patients are lined up in front of the nurses' station for their afternoon drug cocktails. I'm surprised to see Mr. Lions in line, and I decide I'll wait to attempt an interview. A few other patients are in line to get their blood drawn. The phlebotomist—a clean-cut, middle-aged, Asian man wearing thick glasses and blue scrubs—is sitting in a chair behind a small table adjacent to the nurses' station and dutifully drawing a patient's blood. Phlebotomy is one job I'd never want. It's risky, monotonous and deals with two of my least favorite things: blood and needles.

Bored and exhausted, I lean against the wall behind the nurses' station and watch as each patient picks up a Dixie cup full of pills. Mr. Lions is up. Instead of stepping toward the nurses' desk, he moves toward the phlebotomist. He coils back his right arm and makes a fist. Before anyone has a chance to stop him, he punches the phlebotomist in the face. The Asian man falls backward in his chair and blood splatters everywhere. I crouch down behind the nurses' desk, not entirely sure what's going on or what to expect. Someone screams and a nurse yells for security. Blood is all over the floor, and I can't tell if it's from the man's face or the test tubes of patients' blood he's been collecting.

I hear the phlebotomist groan in pain. He's sitting on the floor with his back against the wall. Now I see that his face is covered in blood and his glasses, still over his eyes, are completely smashed. One of the nurses kneels next to him and begins dabbing his face with a moist towel. It feels like a bomb went off.

"Let's get him to the ER!" someone yells.

I slowly get up from my crouched position and see two massive security guards, one on each side of Mr. Lions, grasping his arms and pushing him face first against the wall. Lions isn't resisting at all. He looks like putty in their hands. The head nurse, Marie, charges down the hallway toward the chaos.

"Everyone, please get out of the hallway!" she commands. "We have to file an incident report. Please go back to your rooms or the group room. You can't be here."

I remain motionless behind the nurses' desk for another minute or so as the patients leave, the phlebotomist is led out, and Mr. Lions, looking like a rag doll tethered between two Hulks, is dragged to the Quiet Room, where patients are sent when they misbehave.

I peek inside and cringe. Mr. Lions is lying stiff in the bed with about five people around him. His eyes are closed and he looks heavily sedated. His arms and legs are tied down at his sides by leather restraints. Dr. Patel, wearing latex gloves, is bent over the bed and sticking a syringe in Mr. Lions' leg. Everyone keeps staring at Mr. Lions, whose head starts nodding up and down as if he's fighting to stay awake. He looks like a roped lump of meat and bones under everyone's observation, like a captured alien. My stomach feels uneasy, and even though Mr. Lions punched someone for no reason, I can't help but feel sorry for him.

One thing I like to do is picture the psychiatric patients as carefree, innocent kids and wonder at what point in their journey to adulthood the switch flipped and they went crazy. I wonder if going crazy is as fast as a finger-snap or a gradual process. Maybe it's something programmed deep within our genetic code that we can't keep from happening. It'd be remarkable if we could isolate the exact point someone went from sane to insane.

I stay glued to the window picturing Mr. Lions as a young child; him riding a bike with the neighborhood kids, waking up early on Christmas morning to open presents, and holding his mom's hand while he crosses the street. But seeing him drugged and restrained makes it difficult to imagine him as an innocent, little boy. He doesn't look human. He's a crucified monster.

I manage to drive home without falling asleep at the wheel. Moses is fine and her usual happy self. Chase isn't home, and for a brief moment it doesn't feel like the apartment is a paranoia factory. I could eat dinner, but I'm not that hungry. I could work out, but I'm too tired. I crawl into bed with Moses and fall asleep.

13

I not only slept, but I overslept. I throw on some clothes, wolf down a quick breakfast, make a coffee to go and hurry out the door. Patel will yell at me if I'm late, and it's the last thing my evaluation needs. I hop in my Jeep, blast the radio and roll the windows all the way down. It's sunny and breezy outside, and the air tangling my hair feels freeing. I turn onto the highway, zip 'round and down the circular ramp, and then I hear a loud thud.

My head jerks forward and to the right like someone shoved me from behind. The world suddenly goes sideways. I feel a sharp burning sensation on the insides of my legs that makes me cry out loud. It takes a second to realize that the world is sideways because my Jeep has inexplicably flipped over. And my coffee is no longer inside its cup.

I'm dazed; it was so fast. I shake my head rapidly back and forth to bring some sense into the situation. I look down at my body but nothing feels hurt. Maybe I'm in shock. My lap feels like it's on fire, but I can move. I think about fire and how cars can suddenly burst into flames and command myself to just move and get out of there.

I crawl up and out through the passenger window, quickly survey the damage and half-expect the Jeep to explode. Then I shake my head in wonder. Jesus, I'm lucky there was no traffic. I could have been killed. With my heart pounding, I jog to a gas station and tell them that my car just flipped over. The manager is sympathetic, offers me some coffee, and tells me to take as long as I need. I laugh at the coffee offer considering I'm wearing my old coffee. Once my heart rate feels like it's in the normal range again, I decide I need to call a tow truck, Patel and my school.

I'm not sure why, but before calling the tow service, I dial my parents' number instead. My mom answers the phone and I immediately blurt out the story of the morning's events.

"What?!" she responds. "How did that happen? Is this because of that Chase guy? He had something to do with this!"

I'm taken by surprise. My mom is extremely intuitive. Sure, Chase is a bit paranoid, but how or why would he cause my Jeep to go topsy-turvy?

"No, Mom. I don't think so. I don't know what happened. It all just happened so fast. The important thing," I remind her, "is that I'm not hurt."

"No," she insists. "I don't have a good feeling about this. I'm driving down tonight with your father. We're moving you out tonight. I don't care where you move to, but we're getting you away from that man."

"What?" I cry in complete disbelief. "How am I going to find a place that fast? It wasn't Chase! The Jeep just flipped over! Jeeps...do that," I say, even as I question that premise.

"We're moving you out tonight. That's final," my mom commands.

I surrender, and after saying goodbye, I call the school and tell my program director why I won't be at my clinical rotation today. He assures me that it won't be an issue, he'll notify Patel, and he hopes I'm okay. Then, I call my friend Naomi, tell her what happened, and ask for her help packing boxes later that evening. She agrees and promises to recruit more people. Then I call an apartment complex nearby to see if a studio is available immediately. Miraculously, they have a vacancy. The leasing office tells me I can move in tonight if I come up with a security deposit and the first month's rent. Finally, I call a towing company. They can be there within an hour. It's surreal how everything is falling into place like perfectly positioned dominos.

Naomi calls me back and wants to know all the details. I tell her I don't know how it happened.

"Huh. Chase was in the school library telling everyone that you changed your tire yesterday and did it wrong."

A lump forms in my throat, blocking the air from moving. I feel light-headed, immobilized, like when I try to run in my dreams but can't make my feet move.

"I didn't change my tire," I tell Naomi, finally regaining my voice. "I've never changed a tire in my life. Just tell everyone I'm alright and to be there at four."

I hang up. After an hour of nervously shuffling around the gas station and inhaling fumes, the tow truck arrives. I explain to the friendly driver what happened and he lets out a long, low whistle before motioning for me to hop into his truck. We drive to the wreck and he gets to work. As he's hooking up my unfortunate vehicle to the back of the truck, I ask him what he thinks happened. He says he's not sure, could be a fluke accident. I ask him if someone could have tampered with my tires. He shrugs, tells me it's possible but he can't be certain. I nod and decide that even if it were possible, I don't want to know.

Three hours later, my parents arrive with my oldest sister, a stack of cardboard boxes, and packing tape. We don't say much and immediately start throwing things in boxes. We pack frantically, as if we're evacuating before an impending, deadly storm. In the middle of this, Chase walks in and goes to his room, closing the door.

Naomi, a dark-haired brute of a woman, gets there an hour later. Her coarse face looks focused and her sleeves are rolled up, revealing two masculine arms that appear ready to lift and load. Two other classmates, Beth and Danny, are with her. They immediately join my parents and sister by dutifully tossing my possessions into crates, carrying them out to cars and driving everything over to my new studio apartment. I silently pray it was a family member and not a classmate who packed my underwear and dirty laundry. The whole process is a fatiguing whirlwind.

At nine, my mother and I are standing in the kitchen, packing my silverware. Chase, wearing a white t-shirt and shorts, walks in. He's holding a coffee cup. He seems oddly calm. I don't know what he thinks about this mess. I haven't even told him I'm moving out.

He grabs the coffee pot and pours some into his mug. I wonder how long the coffee has been there. My mother says hello to him and asks if everything's okay. I shoot her a confused glance, but she ignores me. Chase smiles and tells her that he thinks someone is tampering with his computer and breaking into his personal records. My mother listens intently and nods, as if the conversation is perfectly normal. I feel panicked. It's too fake. It needs to stop. Chase takes a few more sips of his cold, stale coffee before saying goodbye and heading back to his room.

"What are you doing, Mom?" I blurt out when I think Chase is safely out of earshot.

"Just trust me," she explains. "I've dealt with these types before and want to make sure he doesn't pull a knife on us. You need to affirm a psychotic person's delusions and go along with them so they don't get angry. You don't want to challenge them."

My mom must be relying on her nursing experience. For years, she was a nurse in a hospital that cared for many psychiatric patients before giving it up to raise us kids. Still, it feels wrong.

"How is he supposed to get better if no one tells him straight up that he's acting like a nutcase?" I yell, anxious and confused. My heart suddenly sinks through the floor. That's when I realize that I also pretended like nothing was wrong with Chase. I could have at least bought him food or convinced him to go to class. I didn't try hard enough. It's too late, and I'm flooded with guilt. My rescuers are forcing me to move on, full steam ahead, and there's no turning back.

Two exhausting hours later, Naomi, Beth and I sit on the floor of my new apartment. I look around and see haphazardly placed boxes and furniture, empty pizza boxes, cookies and diet cola bottles. I'm not looking forward to fixing all this.

I bite into a piece of pizza and tune out Naomi and Beth, who are talking about a movie they both saw. I think of Chase and wonder what he's thinking, what he's doing. My guess is that he's probably pacing up and down the hallway. He paces a lot, like the psych patients and the zoo tigers. I notice crazy people in general pace a lot, as if they are addicted to back and forth motion.

"Chase is a nut job, seriously. A total schizo!" Naomi

exclaims, her manly and authoritative voice booming.

She triggers something inside me. I cringe. "He's just going through a rough time!" I snap. I'm tired and immediately wish I hadn't said anything. I know the rumors already started. Chase is a nut, a schizophrenic, nothing more. He'll probably get kicked out of school and pumped up with pills, but still, I can't call him a schizo. I have too many warm and fond memories of him to ever call him a nutcase. I've witnessed his brilliant, creative wit firsthand, and I refuse to label him something that comes with a slew of negative connotations. Not Chase.

"He tried to kill you, Becka!" Naomi fires back. "He still may try to kill you! And you're defending him? Whatever. It's late. I'm leaving, and you're welcome."

Before I can thank her for helping me move, she storms out of my apartment. Beth follows.

Alone on my floor, I sigh, still thinking of Chase. Part of me wants to run back over to the apartment and hug him, but I know I'll only be embracing a husk of the man I once adored. He's an Old Yeller now, a good dog gone rabid. A brilliant failure who'll eventually get locked up in a ward and kept hidden from the world. And then the big-gun drugs will dim whatever light is left inside of him.

I find my bed and climb in. What a day it's been. My head spins with an overload of sensations. How am I doing all this? I question my own mental health. In the past few weeks I've lost a boyfriend, started antidepressants, binged, purged, drank, been accused of being a hooker, got a massive tattoo, been told I'm borderline borderline, almost died in a car accident, lived with a crazy man, met all types of mentally ill people, and moved. It's a miracle I haven't gone mad.

And then the tears come. Uncontrollably. I hate this hospital and doctor stuff so much. I feel soulless, catatonic. I just want to leave. My emotions feel like shoes stuck in mud and I always have the urge to curl up into a ball, as if my own body is trying to make me disappear. And I don't mind. I want to disappear. I want to leave, but I also feel stuck. What will I do if I leave? I don't think I care anymore. I just need to leave.

PART II

14

I always feel nervous on the turnpike. I'm scared I'll swerve into giant, speeding trucks in the adjacent lanes and get crushed. If I could take back roads to all of my destinations, I would.

It's Monday, the start of my second week of my psychiatry clinical rotation, but I'm not going. The weather is hot and sticky, so I have the windows rolled down. I just dropped Moses off at my parents' house in Easton, Pennsylvania, after telling them I was going to Florida to visit some friends. The Florida trip is a lie. I'm planning to fly to California for absolutely no reason at all. I know my parents would have flipped if I told them the truth.

I'm not sure what I'm going to do in California. All I know is that I feel like a slave to my impulses. I have an impulse to jump on a plane and fly to California, so I'm going. I don't care what I do or what happens out there. I'm just going.

I do care about my cat. She's a precious, black, furry

creature of unerring devotion. She's the most loveable, most alive thing in my life. I know my parents, both extremely caring animal people, will take amazing care of her till I come back.

A tear slides down my face, and I lift my foot off the gas pedal while I rub my eyes. Maybe it's stupid to love a cat so much, but she really is the only thing I can count on in my life. No matter what I thought or did, she never failed to cuddle next to me every night. On the nights I couldn't stand myself, the nights I binged and purged and felt defeated and disappointed in myself, she was always there for me. In this world, you need a cat or a dog to experience unconditional love.

The Philadelphia exit is up ahead so I must have been driving quite fast. As I turn off the turnpike and onto the road heading toward my apartment complex, I pass the usual stores, restaurants, and ASPCA where my oldest sister adopted three of her four cats. I drive in complete silence. I had the radio on earlier, but now singing voices would just bother me. One mile, and then one more.

I make an abrupt, unscheduled left turn, toward my school. I slow down, but my mind is racing. My thoughts used to be boats, just floating along, but now they're motorized. I'm having a hard time keeping up with them. I turn and park, and take a deep breath before walking inside the school. I feel hypnotized by an invisible wand.

The door to the dean's office is cracked open. I peek inside and see Dr. Jacobs, the dean, busily typing at his desk. I knock twice. He looks up, smiles and motions me inside.

"Becka! What brings you here?" He's cheerful, frail, elderly and pale, and he's grinning. His large, stylish glasses make his tiny head look even smaller. He looks like a songbird.

"Hi, Dr. Jacobs. Can I talk to you?"

"Sure. What's up?" he chirps.

I stare at him, trying to gauge how serious I am about the words making their way out of my mouth. "Well… actually, I'm here to quit school."

He looks stunned. He starts to say something but stops. He leans forward, crosses his arms and stares at me. "Is something wrong, Becka? Why on earth would you quit? You're a good student. You passed your Boards. Do you mean that you need a leave of absence?"

"No. No, really, I quit," I say more forcefully. "I know I'm doing okay, but I…I just really don't want to be here anymore."

"But…Becka! That's not a good decision. You have loans to pay back. I think you'd make a great doctor someday. Why not see the school psychiatrist?"

"I already saw a shrink, and I'm already on drugs."

"Drugs?"

"Prescribed, sorry. I'm on an antidepressant. A shrink

gave me one weeks ago. But, sorry, I made up my mind. I appreciate what you're trying to do here, but I've made my decision. I just don't want to do this anymore. At all." Splashes of tears hit my denim-clad legs. He pushes a box of tissues on his desk toward me. I grab two and blow my nose.

"What will you do? Do you know what you're going to do?" he pleads softly.

California, I think. For no good reason at all. "No. I don't know yet," is my response.

"Becka," he implores, leaning in closer, "you're going to regret this decision." Regret is one of those words that usually hits my gut like a dagger and makes me want to rethink a decision. This time it doesn't.

"I'm sure. Positive. Thank you." As I turn my back on him, I glance back and see his expression. I've seen it before. He thinks I've lost my mind. And maybe he's right. Maybe I'm going where Chase has gone, to the Manic Kingdom of Spellbound Lunatics – return flights, unknown.

I know this sensation: I'm walking away from something big. It feels like I just broke up with someone I'm still in love with, like I'm purposely breaking my own heart. Self-sabotage seems to be my latest hobby, because it satiates me. I hate where I am and what I'm doing. I'm tired of merely holding on and going through the motions like a puppet on a string. Today, I'm cutting the strings, even though I might want them back tomorrow.

15

It's Tuesday, early morning, and still dark outside. I'm on a chilly, damp plane to Los Angeles and stuck in the dreaded middle seat. A fat balding man has the aisle and a petite Asian woman is tucked in the prized window seat. I drank a few glasses of wine before leaving, so thankfully I'm able to hide in my oversized grey-hooded sweatshirt and sleep for the first half of the trip.

I'm up and awake for the second bumpy half of the flight. Bored, I curiously spy on the other passengers, read a few magazines, and think a lot. I think about ex-boyfriends, my unplanned trip to Los Angeles, quitting school, being depressed, suicidal ideations, and whether or not I'm crazy. Random memories flash in my mind like a carelessly put-together scrap book. Just another pointless cerebral search for causes and meanings.

Suddenly, the pilot announces that we'll be landing soon. Upon hearing the news, the fat man, the Asian woman, and I simultaneously squirm like mealworms and stretch in our seats. The fat man obnoxiously sneezes, landing a few sticky drops on the side of my neck. I cringe but don't wipe them off right away. I'm distracted by the Asian woman who starts frantically digging in her oversized black purse, pulling out a handful of tissues and holding them up to cover her mouth and nostrils, as if allowing in another molecule of air will kill her instantly. Her eyes are wild and frightened. They bulge even further when the obese man sneezes again. I can't help but snicker. If paranoia isn't the opposite of apathy, I don't know what is.

I pick up my suitcase at the baggage claim and take a cab to Lanes, the hotel I booked. It's the perfect beach-side getaway, and it's spacious and clean, my two major hotel room requirements. My room has a balcony overlooking the beach and a snow-white, king-size bed, upon which I plop and sigh. The back of my head sinks slowly into the fluffy white pillows while my back and limbs fall limp against the comfortable mattress. The sinking feeling is a heavenly relief. I feel like I'm floating on a raft and wish I could perpetually descend into the enticing bed and hide forever. I want to burrow into oblivion. I want to fizzle out like a wet firecracker.

I roll over and check the hotel alarm clock; it's 10 AM. The California sun is peeking through the dusty retro curtains hanging from the window and shining directly on my face. It's coaxing me to go outside. Since it's still early morning, I figure I should go for a run and get a feel for my surroundings. I push myself out of bed, dig in my suitcase for my rescue inhaler, and take two puffs to stave off any impending asthma attacks. I hate my lungs.

After I'm clothed in a red tank top, black mesh running shorts, and sneakers, I rub sunscreen on every bit of pale, exposed skin. I take baby powder and apply it liberally over my body, rubbing the extra on my shorts. Baby powder seems to prevent heat rash, a slew of tiny red, hideous-looking bumps that sprout everywhere after a long, sweaty run. I hate my white skin.

I open the curtains wider and take in the view. There are a few people, some with dogs, strolling along the boardwalk. The ocean, only a short, sandy distance beyond, is calm and looks like a grey, sparkly cloth waiting to envelop eager swimmers. The scene almost excites me, though I haven't been excited in so long that I forget what excitement feels like. My feelings of excitement are much like that of the residual, neuronal activity of a dead person. They come in twitches.

After a quick elevator ride, I exit through the rear of the hotel. I cross a narrow paved path where more people dressed in bright beach clothes are rollerblading and riding bicycles. A small wooden hut along the tiny path rents bikes to tourists, and there's a tiny stand next to that renting out surfboards. An outdoor gym is directly behind the hotel on the opposite side of the paved path. There are climbing ropes, monkey bars, swings, pull-up bars and other outdoor exercise props set up in the sand around a square-shaped plot of verdant grass. A gravel track loops around the perimeter of the lush lawn. A few people are facing the ocean with meditative gazes, sitting on park benches randomly planted in the sand. A little closer to the water, children with plastic shovels and pails are vainly trying to build stable sand castles. There's nothing uninviting about the atmosphere.

I start kicking my way through the sand in an effort to get loosened up for a run, but I still feel like an unmotivated pile of mush. I decide to stretch first so I walk over to one of the metal horizontal bars and place my left leg on top of it. I stretch, allowing my head to fall down and meet my lower leg, which I kiss. I'm extremely flexible and figure the moment I can no longer kiss my leg is the moment I'm either too fat or too old.

As I stretch, I close my eyes. My ears are drowning in a collage of sound waves chaotically constructed with children's laughter, bird songs, breezes, and other unidentifiable clangs and bangs when a deep, strong masculine voice from somewhere behind me asks, "Is that a tattoo?"

16

I awkwardly swing my leg up and off the bar and clumsily turn around. A shirtless, massive black man who is damn good looking is sitting on a bench behind me and hoggishly eating some kind of food with one hand while drenching it with a bottle of hot sauce from the other. His naked toes are dug into the sand and in between his feet is a large paper bag that looks like it might be a brown-bagged breakfast for a monster. I notice a black bag on the bench by his side and a black sweatshirt draped over it. He appears to be alone and has an air of pointlessness about him. That, combined with his over-used, wrinkled and stained brown bag makes me think he's a homeless bum, but a handsome homeless bum.

I figure that while I was bent over stretching, the bottom half of my tank top separated just enough from my waist band for him to catch a glimpse of my tattoo. Normally, I'd ignore him, walk away and start running. The man seems frighteningly strange. But I haven't talked to anyone in a while, so what the heck. I smile at the man and say, "Yes. It's a tattoo."

"Nice. I like ink. Why'd you get it?" he asks nonchalantly, licking his fingers of mystery victuals doused with Tabasco.

I think for a moment, staring past him to gaze blankly at the backside of my hotel. I wonder if I should tell him I'm trying to fight death with permanency, that I'm crazy and the tattoo was a temporary reprieve against morbid stagnation.

"You're daydreaming," he notes with utter confidence.

"Oh, sorry. I do that a lot lately. I like ink, too. That's why," I finally answer. I don't sound nearly as confident as he.

He stands up, and on his feet, he looks gigantic and formidable. He's about six feet, two inches, and well over two hundred pounds of finely chiseled muscle. All he's wearing is a pair of navy blue swim trunks and a few stubborn sand particles stuck to his calves. When he stretches his arms up to the sky, easily showing off his well-built shoulders, he reminds me of a bear. Each of his abdominal muscles is clearly visible and protrudes proudly. His torso is smooth and hairless and I get the feeling he has the potential for Herculean strength. His belly button is a prominent outie, which makes me giggle. This man's brown bulge for a belly button is so big that it looks like a game show buzzer. I'm half-tempted to run over and push it.

"I'm King, by the way," he says, and laughs. "Did you get in a doughnut fight this morning?"

I bite my lip and look down to keep from laughing. He has the physical stature and poise of a king, but his name sounds made-up, and a little ridiculous.

"I'm Becka. Um...doughnut fight?"

He moves closer to me. My heart speeds up. Instantly, I feel even smaller and more insignificant than before. He's a giant. He looks like he works out all day, every day. He gestures toward my running clothes. I look down and see I'm covered in white powder.

"Oh!" I exclaim, chuckling nervously. "No, no doughnuts. That's baby powder."

He raises an eyebrow in response and inches closer. I stumble backwards. I don't feel like talking anymore. He's too close to me, and it's making me anxious. I want to start running. Let him think what he wants. He won't matter to me in five minutes.

"So what brings you out this way?" he asks.

I softly sigh. He must have nothing better to do. "Just a vacation."

"You and every other girl who comes out here. So, where ya from?"

"Pennsylvania."

"P-A!" he guffaws, slapping his thigh. "My dad went to school there. U Penn. He was a Fulbright Scholar."

"Oh. Very cool." All I want to do is go for a run along the water and get high on my endorphins, not discuss fatherly alumni.

"So what do you do in P-A, Miss Becka?" he presses.

I'm getting frustrated and start rocking back and forth on my feet. He's way too friendly. I don't want to give him my whole life story or delve into my recent string of self-destruction. He hasn't earned the truth. I tell myself that fibbing to a stranger during brief encounters is perfectly acceptable, especially if it will get me out of this awkward situation.

"I'm a med student," I state impatiently. It's not a total lie. I'm only a recent drop-out.

"A med student?" he exclaims. His brown eyes grow larger. "Wow, now that's great – and impressive. You must be sharp! There are some doctors in my family back in Nigeria. In fact, my father owns two hospitals in Lagos, Nigeria. Any idea what kind of doctor you want to be?"

His compliments make me feel like a huge let-down. It hurts to hear them. They don't apply to me anymore.

"No," I softly mumble.

"That's okay. You have plenty of time. So, before medical school, where did you study?" It's apparent he has nothing else to do today but talk to me.

"A military school. It was different," I say quickly. I wonder if he can see my feet dancing. I'm ready to run.

"That's even more impressive!" He grins, in awe. "You don't look like the type."

"Yeah, I get that a lot."

"A soldier girl, huh? Well, I like that."

I nod and back away. He moves toward me as he ignores all hints. "How was it being a soldier?"

"Hard and complicated by asthmatic lungs," I snap this time.

"Oh."

I know I sound bitter, but I always sound bitter when I tell people about my asthma. I came down with a severe atypical pneumonia years ago. My friends wanted me to go to the hospital, but I refused. Instead, when my trachea's diameter felt like it decreased by half, I drank tons of coffee, since caffeine is a natural bronchodilator. The infection gradually resolved, but in the aftermath I developed asthma. Now, every time I run or get upset, it feels like my lungs are collapsing. Sometimes I can barely breathe. A shrink told me it was all anxiety-related, but my internal medicine doctor diagnosed me with asthma and prescribed me both a rescue inhaler and steroid inhaler. My running's never been the same, but even worse than that is crying, which can quickly trigger my asthma. Getting upset somehow makes my bronchioles fill up with inflammatory crud and collapse. It doesn't happen every time I cry, but when it does, it's awful. So awful, I try not to cry over anything. Before this hit me, I didn't even know it was possible to be allergic to tears.

"You have asthma and you're going for a run?" King seems concerned.

"I already used my inhaler in the hotel. I'm good to go."

"Hotel? Where are you staying?"

"Right there," I answer while pointing to Lanes behind him. It's time to divert attention away from myself. All these questions are making me uncomfortable, so I turn the tables and ask one of my own. "So, what do you do?"

Without hesitation, King enthusiastically answers, "I'm a lawyer. My office is here in Santa Monica. I live in Venice. I have two homes in Venice. I mostly work pro bono now, though."

"Oh." I nod, trying to hide my surprise. I thought he was a beach bum, literally. I tell myself to start filtering my first impressions of people. Clearly, I'm way off. Or he's lying. Either way, who cares.

King interrupts my self-assessment. "Can I see your tattoo? It looked pretty big from where I was sitting before. I love ink. It's the sexiest thing on a woman."

I nod, turn and slightly lift my shirt while pulling the waistband of my shorts away from my back so King can see my full tattoo. Even as I look away, I feel him staring intensely at my back and can see him extending his neck, as if he's trying to see more of my body. I feel nervous and ashamed, like I've shown him too much. I pull my shirt back down and make a motion toward the water when King says, "It's really, really nice. Music notes? Do you play an instrument?"

"Yes," I bark and wish I never said hello to this man. "I play the violin."

King looks impressed again. It's so easy to impress him. He starts rambling about the origin of the violin. Then he starts talking about a famous violin recently stolen from somewhere up in San Francisco. I keep nodding but tune him out. It feels like he wants to talk to me all day.

Minutes later, I'm still nodding and he's still rambling, jumping from one topic to the next. He speaks eloquently with big words and his voice is smooth and refined, as if his vocal cords are trained for making distinguished conversation. One could easily call him charming, possibly one of the most charming men I've ever met.

His charm, charisma, whatever you want to call it, feels off, though. His words and mannerisms seem rehearsed, like a salesman's, like he's given this random speech to a thousand girls before me in this exact spot. I'm not interested in what he's saying, but I automatically pick up that he went to NYU for law school, was raised in Brooklyn and decided to move out to California to practice law. He also works out twice a day and works as a writer in his spare time.

"What do you write?" I interrupt.

"Screenplays." He's nonchalant.

"Anything big? Anything I'd know?"

"Not yet. But I'm working on a tragic one about the mobs in Atlantic City and Philadelphia."

"Oh. Neat." I have no interest in mob history. My enthusiasm for this conversation has dropped well below zero. "Well, I'm going to start my run now. It's been nice chatting with you."

"Okay!" he eagerly responds. "Do you want to grab a coffee sometime while you're out here? Can I get your phone number?"

I sigh, audibly. I always have trouble telling a guy that I'm not interested in pursuing anything with him. To avoid that uncomfortable confrontation, I usually give them my number and hope that they don't call, or if they start calling me, they stop calling once I never answer. I wish I could be straightforward and tell a guy I'm not interested, but I can't. And since I can't, I cause myself a lot of undue phone harassment and hassle. As I listen to myself clearly recite my digits to King, I wonder if my inability to openly reject people and the subsequent drama are all part of my big plan to sabotage myself.

King puts my phone number in his cell phone, which further supports his claim that he's a working lawyer and not a homeless man. I figure homeless people don't have actively functioning cell phones. He then gives me his number, which I plug in my phone to be polite. He promises me that he'll call. I nod, hoping he doesn't. I wave and start jogging toward the shore line, convinced I'll never see or talk to him again.

Back in my hotel room, I'm startled when my phone rings. I turned it on when I went running, but for the most part, I keep it off and pretend it doesn't exist. I don't want the temptation to listen to concerned voicemails from friends, professors, and family members. Or worse yet, accusatory messages from Chase. I want to forget he even exists. I luck out this time. It's my college roommate Haley who I haven't spoken to in forever. She has been living and working for the Army in South Korea.

"Becka!" Haley yells into the phone. "What are you doing? I'm in Savannah for a leadership conference for seven more days. It was last minute. Come to Savannah this weekend? I need you to come."

"Um. I'm kinda broke. Actually, I am broke." My bank account full of loan money is rapidly dwindling. It doesn't faze me, though it should. It's not like I have a backup plan for making more money. I shrug and tell myself I'll figure it out later. Nothing fazes me. "Why do you need me?"

"Because I haven't seen you in forever, and it's a short flight from Philly. It'll be fun!!"

"Well," I say, knowing full well I should refuse, "Okay. I guess. Let me see how much tickets are."

"Yay! Call me when you buy your ticket." Haley exclaims.

I hop online and check flights from California to Savannah. Haley assumes I'll be flying in from Philadelphia, but who cares. The less she knows, the better. I absolutely shouldn't buy a ticket, but I do. Maybe hanging out with Haley will remind me of my old self and fix me, or something. Besides, I only booked my California stay till Friday morning. I might as well relax at the beach until Friday and then fly to Savannah. And then...I'll figure that out later.

17

It's Friday, and I'm on a plane en route to Savannah, lucking out with the coveted window seat. While zooming by clouds that look like giant marshmallows, I scold myself for my recent travel binge. It makes me feel even more out of control. I also berate myself for being so easily persuaded by Haley. The girl has my number and knows it. Of course, there's a reason for the soft spot. I witnessed her come to terms with being a lesbian while at military school, and because no one can be openly gay there, it was one of the most emotionally traumatizing experiences I've seen a person go through.

From that moment, I became her eternal wing-woman and started accompanying her to "gay" things, since no one else would. I still cringe just thinking about that time. Many friends ditched her. Her own mother called our barracks room every night, preaching the evils of homosexuality and reciting Bible verses over the phone. Haley sat at her desk, listening, and was convinced she was Hell-bound. Once her mom hung up, I'd try to convince her that she wasn't going to Hell for being gay. It got to be too much for her.

After one of these phone calls, Haley ran up eight flights of stairs to the barracks' roof and was set on jumping off. I ran after her and talked her down, and still that night haunts me. I still feel like I have a duty to protect her and remind her that it's perfectly okay to be herself and nothing more.

The pilot's voice jars me from my flashback by announcing we'll be landing in ten minutes. I stretch, yawn and start mentally preparing for a long night out with Haley. I'll probably need a couple of Red Bulls.

After a bumpy landing, I leave the airport and walk outside to a warm and sunny day. I look around for Haley when a horn honks.

"Becka!" I see a hand waving from the driver's window of a parked maroon car. Haley jumps out of the driver's seat and hugs me. It feels good. I let go and step back to take a better look at her. She's still a pale girl with jet-black hair, squinty eyes, and a blank stare that makes her look eternally stoned. I love her look. She's even skinnier than I remember, but she seems happy, so I decide not to pry about her eating habits. She seems extraordinarily put-together, actually, which makes my smile bigger. It gives me chills, too. She had a suicidal mindset but was able to overcome it, and now I can commiserate.

We hop in the car, and Haley starts driving toward

downtown Savannah. She tells me that we'll be staying at her friend's house, who is out of town. "I'm so happy you came down! No one else will do gay stuff with me. But I promise we'll do 50% gay stuff and 50% straight stuff," Haley declares.

"Yeah right, Haley. I don't really care. We can do 100% gay," I answer while staring out the passenger window. It really is a beautiful day.

Since Haley's coming-out, we often planned outings based on percentages of time allotted for her gay events and the percentage of time reserved for straight events. Usually, due to Haley's still eager sexual discovery and self-centered nature, our time together revolves one hundred percent around her lesbian desires. Sometimes I complain, but this time, I'm content with doing whatever, as long as I don't have to talk about me.

After a light lunch, we drive to Haley's friend's house. It's quaint, dusty, and old-fashioned. She leads me upstairs to a clean, spacious bedroom. "The guest room. This is where we have to sleep," Haley says.

She sits on one edge of the bed and bounces up and down. I nod and plop down on the other side of the bed. We both decide to take a nap before the night's adventure.

By the time we wake up, it's dark out. Haley and I shower, get dressed and load back into the maroon car. While driving, she informs me that we're going to a popular lesbian club. She also praises a drag queen show we're going to see. I nod with fake excitement.

At the club, we sit at a table near the back of a dimly lit room that smells like cigarettes and moth balls. The crowd is big, talkative and butch. There's a tiny stage up front with scarlet-red velvet curtains that occasionally jostle from side to side. I can see feet buckled in fancy, glittery heels zipping to and fro underneath the stage curtains. Haley signals a waitress over and orders us drinks. A few minutes later, the waitress brings us two large glasses. My drink is pink. I'm not sure what it is, but I start guzzling it through a straw. It's strong and sweet.

The stage curtains open and colorful streams of light start maniacally flashing around the room while a man caked in makeup steps center stage. He's wearing a woman's blonde wig and a blue sequined bikini. The crowd erupts into cheers as he lip-syncs "It's Raining Men."

I drink some more while large women wearing flannel shirts and acid-washed jeans eagerly waddle to the front of the stage and begin waving dollar bills in the air. The drag queen delicately bends down toward their smiling heads framed with fierce mullets, pecks them on their pudgy cheeks, and slickly plucks dollar bills from their hands. I glance over at Haley, whose eyes are mesmerized by the events on stage.

"I don't get this. These are men. I thought you liked women?" I whisper loudly to Haley.

She quickly disregards me with a flap of her right hand. "Shh, Becka. This is what gay people do. You breeders wouldn't understand."

I shrug and continue drinking. I drink until the sea of mullets collecting in front of the stage blurs into a giant octopus. I feel myself getting warm and flirty while belting out power ballad lyrics. Soon I'm swaying and feel the urge to kiss any cheek in my visual field. Stumbling to my feet, I grab a dollar bill from the table top, maneuver to the front of the stage, and wave the bill in the air. A hazy drag queen wearing a black, see-through dress kneels in front of me. I smile as he kisses me, takes the bill, and whispers, "Thank you, baby." I giggle from all the drunk, sexual energy surrounding the stage and high-five a talking mullet standing next to me. The talking mullet starts dancing with me and grinding against my jeans. It blows on my neck. I giggle again.

"I'm not gay," I shout, slurring.

"Tonight you are!" the talking mullet says.

I giggle, and the mullet's touching my hair now. I can smell its sweet shampoo. Suddenly, I think of Haley. I look around and can't see her. I trip while dancing and decide to wander outside for a bit. I'm getting hot and have a foggy intuition that I'm too drunk. I make my way to the front door and trip again. Once outside, I breathe in the cool, night air and lean against a random brick building. I see a blurry group of beefy men with identical short haircuts.

They are strutting down the street and howling like a pack of intoxicated wolves. One shouts something at me. The others laugh.

Taking a few more deep breaths, I reach in my pocket and feel my cell phone. I want to call someone. I'm absolutely overwhelmed with the urge to call someone. I browse through my list of contacts. They all look blurry and weird. Then, I look at recent calls and see King's area code. I laugh, remembering how aggressive he was about meeting for coffee. I dial his number and giggle. The phone rings, and rings, and rings.

"Hello, Becka." His voice is smooth and deep. It turns me on.

"Heyyyy," I manage to mumble with gusto. "How did you know it was me?"

King laughs heartily. "I saved your number, of course. I knew you were going to call me. I saw the way you were looking at me."

I laugh and start rambling about being drunk at a drag queen show, until I hear a woman's voice on the phone in the background. It makes my stomach sink. He's with a girl.

"Who is that?" I ask. I know I sound jealous, even though I have absolutely no reason to be jealous. The guy is probably a gigolo anyhow.

"One of my many women!" King confidently replies. "You know I can't have just one. I have a big appetite. Her name's Lila. She's a dancer. We're here at my crib."

I force a laugh. "Let me talk to her." I want to talk to the girl. I want to see what she's made of. I hear King laughing. His laughter is smooth, rhythmic, sexy.

"You want to talk to her? Okay. She's getting ready to go dance somewhere. Tell her to dance for me. See if you can convince her."

Then I don't hear anything. It makes me nervous. Maybe they're kissing. Maybe they're together. I can't know. I hear a scraping noise. It sounds like he dropped the phone and is scrambling to pick it up.

"Yeah?" an annoyed female voice says.

"Lila!" I exhort, dragging out my consonants. "Dance for King! C'mon!"

"Okay," Lila replies in an irritated tone. "I have to go to work. Whoever you are, here's King. I'm leaving."

King gets back on the phone and asks with a deeper, even sexier voice, "You drunk?"

"Yep. I drank way too much tonight."

"Are you horny?" King sounds too eager.

I laugh and don't answer right away. "No. Not really. Just really tipsy. I'm at a gay bar. I have to find my friend. She's somewhere around here. Sorry, I don't know why I called you."

"I do. Do you like women?" King asks with a gleeful voice.

"No," I quickly reply. "Not like that." I laugh again. He's

making me nervous.

I mumble a few more nonsensical sentences when King interrupts me and says, "Hold the phone up to you. Hold it up to your pants. I want to hear you purr. I want to hear how much you want me."

I frown, trying to grasp King's request. My brain is fuzzy. I don't understand it, and though I sense it's an inappropriate remark, I'm drunk and an easy target for ridiculous suggestions. His voice has a calming effect on my body which makes me eager to please him. I slowly lower the phone from my ear and press it up against my inner thigh. I feel a single shivering pulse in my pants as I curl my toes inside my sneakers.

Someone angrily yells out my name. Then again. "Becka!" I hear a woman's voice scream. "Where the hell have you been? I've been looking for you for the past hour! I want pizza."

The blurry girl with the angry voice walks closer to me. She's wearing tight jeans, a white wife-beater and her jet-black hair is tied back in a ponytail, but I don't recognize her. My eyelids feel like two dumbbells drooping heavily toward the ground when the girl violently shakes my left shoulder. I stretch my eyes open wide and realize the girl is Haley. I shake my head back and forth, stand up straighter, put my phone in my pocket and say, "My jean jacket. I have to find my jean jacket."

The next thing I remember is waking up in bed with Haley next to me. It's dark around me. I'm fully dressed and my jean jacket is tied firmly around my waist. Haley's asleep but keeps kicking her legs underneath a soft white sheet we're sharing. I hear a vibrating noise that's coming from Haley's side of the bed.

"Haley," I grumble. "That better be your phone vibrating."

Haley shifts farther away from me on the bed while moaning sleepily. I start to feel around the blankets for my phone. I always lose my cell phone in beds. Finally, my wandering hand hits it under the covers. I have a text message from King. It reads, "Meet me in the morning. You won't regret it!"

I laugh and let out a slightly regretful sigh once I remember calling him. Still, it feels good to receive male attention from someone who is honestly interested in me. I can't crush the notion that King intrigues me on some level, and I haven't felt intrigued in a long time. He makes me want to get out of bed and go see him, and I crave anything and anyone that gets me to move. Maybe that sounds desperate. Maybe I am. But I figure it's okay to meet him for a coffee; he's a sharp-witted, funny lawyer and a fitness guru. I could at least work out with him and get in shape. My intent isn't to date him or fall in love. It's just that I don't have anything else to do. Not one damn thing. And the California sunshine felt so good. Being away from everything familiar felt so good, and I can afford a few more nights in a hotel. I decide to change my return flight from Savannah to California instead of Pennsylvania. Why the heck not?

18

After two alcohol-fueled days in Savannah, I'm back on a plane to Los Angeles. I had a good time with Haley, but there was too much booze. I puked last night and woke up with a pulsing headache that has subsided only a little since boarding the plane. Haley was drunk most of the time, too. I used to get irritated when she got drunk, but this time I was grateful, because she lacked the cerebral capacity to ask me any probing questions and figure out I was in a bad place. Gratitude is weird, I think, as the plane lands softly in Los Angeles.

After a thirty minute cab ride, I arrive at a hotel a few streets over from Lanes. The hotel's not posh, but it's not cheap, either. After checking into my room, I dive onto one of the beds. Then I turn over on my back, stare at the plain white ceiling and start thinking. I still have a faint headache and feel a little dizzy. Attempting to make it stop, I slam my eyes shut, but that only makes me dizzy in the dark. I open my eyes again, but now the hotel furniture feels like it's doing a circular dance around me. I close my eyes again and start taking deep breaths, hoping the spinning feeling stops soon. King is supposed to call me when he's through with his morning workout. It's 11 AM, so I figure he'll call soon. In the meantime, I have to fight this dizziness and avoid thinking, since that just makes it worse. And it never works. I'm a thought machine. I think about my parents and how no one knows I'm in California. I think about my cat and wonder if she misses me. I think about my full voicemail box. I start questioning my decision to fly back to California and invite King to my hotel room. My breathing quickens and my left eye starts twitching, all of which seems to make my headache worse. I instantly consider calling the whole thing off and flying home.

The ringing phone interrupts my thoughts. I feel relieved and answer it. It's a cheerful, hospitable female voice, the kind that make me feel envious, speaking from the front desk. She tells me that a gentleman by the name of King is here to see me. I take a deep breath and tell her I'll meet him in the lobby.

On my feet, I feel a little less dizzy. I inhale and exhale deeply as I slowly walk down the bright hotel hallway toward the elevator. I have on the same outfit I flew here in, a black tank top, fluorescent blue running shorts, and flip flops. My hair is tied back in a messy bun. I stare at my anemic feet while panic ambushes my mind. Still, I keep walking toward the elevator as if an invisible force with an invisible magic wand is making me. I hear the elevator's bell, and the doors glide open. I hear a deep voice call my name.

My eyes drift from the floor to King as he steps out of the elevator. Immediately, I wish I had never invited him to my hotel. He has a frantic, desperate look of excitement on his chocolate face. His massive frame is barely clad in blue shorts, a white t-shirt, and basketball high tops. The same tattered black bag I saw him with the first time we met hangs from his right shoulder. In his left hand is a large brown paper bag, speckled with greasy smudge marks. Everything, his eyes, expression and body language, makes me feel like prey about to be swallowed. I silently beg for something to happen that will make him step back in the elevator and go away. Some part of me hopes this is only a bad dream.

I inhale deeply to calm the exploding nerves in my gut. I can't ask him to go away. That would create a massively uncomfortable conflict, so I remind myself that he intrigued me, and I haven't felt interested in anyone or anything in a long time. I start to feel better, or at least less sick.

I force myself to give him a quick, sweaty hug and he hugs me back. It's a quick, awkward embrace, a physical reminder of how unsure we are of each other. I gesture for him to follow me down the hallway to my room. He starts bantering, but I can't listen to him. He's walking behind me and my knees go weak. What if he's a serial killer? What if I'm about to die? What if he grabs me by the neck from behind? I completely tune him out and contemplate ways to get him to leave.

"Oh, God!" I didn't mean to let that slip.

"What?" King asks, a look of complete surprise on his face.

"Nothing," I reply while shaking my head back and forth. It's too late now. I can't turn back. Besides, I'm letting my imagination get the best of me.

I slide the hotel card key in my door and push it open as King flings his bags to a corner in the room and tightly grabs me behind my waist. I nervously laugh as my heart starts galloping. I free myself from his grasp, sit down on the bed, and watch as he removes his shirt, and then his shorts. He stands naked in front of me with starvation in his eyes and an erection so large that I feel immediately sick to my stomach. I feel like a scrumptious buffet in front of a famished African village. I'm going to vomit.

"Um," I half whimper, half speak. "I don't feel good. I feel... I don't feel right."

King chuckles. He slowly approaches the bed and pushes my shoulders backward with his monstrous hands. He gently straddles me. I look him in the eye.

"Be gentle," I whisper.

He nods but I don't think he heard me. I turn my head to the side and close my eyes. I don't want eye contact, nor do I want to kiss him. Kissing means trust, real kissing means love. This is using each other. This is hedonism. This is intrigue. This is not love. Love and intimacy take time. They're feelings that naturally blossom between two people who do a lot of things together and go through a lot of shit together over a lot of time. Sex doesn't even factor into the equation, and I'm not one of those girls who has a problem distinguishing sex from love.

King tries turning my head toward his, but I snap it back in the opposite direction. He tries again, and this time I verbalize firmly. "No!"

He gets the hint, pushes his body up and farther from mine and closes his eyes. Even though I don't want to be intimate with him, I feel like I need him. I need him as a distraction from everything that's wrong with me. For the moment, he's a breathing jigsaw puzzle that occupies my mind and keeps me from giving in to my dismal thoughts. As he rhythmically maneuvers his body, I feel for his prominent belly button. I slide my hand underneath his stomach and firmly press on it, like the game-show buzzer I imagined when I first saw him. Let the game begin!

"I'm the best," King murmurs, through deep breathing. "I'm the best there is. I'm the best there is and the best there ever was!"

I bite my tongue and suppress my laughter while King continues talking like he's Muhammad Ali of the bedroom. I want to laugh, because he's delusional. He's selfish and feels as sensual as a toilet plunger. For the last couple of minutes, I feel like a pile of pig slop being attacked by a giant heifer. I close my eyes tighter and silently wish for him to hurry and finish before he does something dangerous like pierce my lungs.

I open my eyes briefly. His eyes are closed. His head moves slightly from side to side. He's breathing heavily and sweating now. I close my eyes again. With both of our eyes closed and two wandering imaginations, it's like we aren't even with each other. Part of me wonders who he's thinking of. Part of me doesn't care.

His arms lock into place. His face quivers violently. Spasms ripple across his glistening torso while his breath seems trapped in his throat. His eyes open. He looks beyond me to the headboard for a few seconds and then closes his eyes again. He takes a few short breaths and then rolls over and sighs. "Whoa. Oh, man, that was great. I just came thinking about two lesbians I had not too long ago."

I look away, yawn and shift over toward the opposite side of the bed.

"How was that for you?" he asks, though I'm not sure why since he's convinced he's a bedroom god.

"Great," I lie.

"You really came hard," he says drowsily.

"Yep." The lies come easier than I do.

"I'm gonna take a nap. Want to order food when I get up?"

"Sure." I curl up in the fetal position and shift away from him. I feel the tears in my eyes. I feel like dirt. I don't want to wake up.

19

King and I make "love" again in the late afternoon. It's a little better the second time around. At least, I start to feel more comfortable and less dizzy. When we're done, I crawl to the other side of the bed. He holds out his arm and says, "Honey. Come here. Why are you so afraid of being close?"

I freeze. I never expected him to ask that. Usually they don't care. I don't know how to answer his question, so I shrug and crawl over to his outstretched arm. He kisses my head and holds me tight. He flips on the television with his free arm and begins channel surfing.

"I haven't watched TV in years. It seems like it's only trash," he comments while continuing to change channels.

"In years? That's a long time. You don't watch TV at your place?"

"No. It's a waste. Nothing good is on. Plus, most of my things are in storage," King says while stroking my hair.

"Storage? Why?" I ask, thinking I need a nap. I'm always so tired. It has to be those darn happy pills. I guess if you're asleep, you can't be depressed.

"Selling one place. Finishing another. It was just easier that way."

"Oh," I answer, not caring enough to ask for more details. "So... two lesbians? When did you see two lesbians?"

King snorts. "Oh, God. They were crazy. It was about two weeks ago. They came to town and started chatting me up on the beach. We partied that night, all night long. One was brunette, the other a redhead. Yeah, they wore me out, those two."

"So you hooked up with both of them at the same time?" My tone's ripe with disgust and jealousy.

"Yes, honey. I told you I like pink," King comments nonchalantly.

"I know, I know. It's just... weird to me, that's all."

"What's weird about it?"

I don't say anything for a minute or two. The honest answer is that I'm kind of disgusted and a little repulsed, but afraid of starting an argument. I answer with, "It's just... I guess, different, is all."

"You think too much," King tells me. "I'm starving. Do you want to order food? Want Thai? I'm hungry for Thai."

"Sure," I agree.

My mind shifts from lesbian hookups to my hungry stomach. I can definitely eat, and Thai is as good as any. King pulls his arm out from under me and finds a Thai menu from the bedstand drawer. He asks what I want, saying it's his treat, and I say something low fattening and vegetarian. Then he asks me to look in his black bag for money.

"Where should I look?" I ask him once I'm crouched down in the corner of the room and about to dig through his bag.

"Front pocket. There should be a bag of money in there."

I stick my hand in the front pocket and pull out a Ziploc bag. Inside are three twenty dollar bills, King's driver's license and a Vons grocery card.

"Is this it?" I ask while holding up the plastic bag.

"Yep. Grab a twenty, that should cover it."

"You don't have a wallet?"

"Nah. The bag works fine. I don't keep change, and I can see everything this way."

I shrug, figuring King's just an eccentric guy who's going to do things his way regardless of the norm. Maybe he's on the run from some horrible crime. He could still be a serial killer but just decided not to kill me. Yet. Oh, God. I feel butterflies in my stomach again and literally slap myself out of becoming a tremoring idiot.

Thirty minutes later, the food arrives. We both shovel it in silently without talking. Once King is done, he leans back against a pillow on the bed and claims he's extremely tired. He yawns and tells me he's going to get up the next morning at 5:30 AM to work out, and if I want, I can meet him at the workout spot (where we first met) when I wake up. I agree to meet him there some time in the morning. He mumbles good night, kisses me on the cheek, and goes to sleep. Lying down next to him, I drift into a light sleep.

King's loud, staccato snoring wakes me. I roll over on my side so I can face him and stare at his giant chocolate frame. Years ago, I never would have predicted that I would be lying in bed with a black man. I'm not racist, I just happened to grow up in a tiny town populated with the white descendants of coal miners and few to none black people. I never thought I would date a black man, because I never saw one.

While still staring at King, I wonder if we'll have enough sex to alter the chemicals in my brain for me to fall in love with him. It's all chemical after all. And when enough chemicals are involved, we'll call it love. We might even call each other soul-mates. I want to believe in a little magic, but I don't. Of course, I'm also depressed.

King continues to vigorously snore like a beast in deep slumber one wouldn't want to disturb. Still lying in bed, I take a deep breath and smell the aroma of fresh hotel sex. It makes me feel used and guilty. I roll over in the bed, farther away from him, and try to sleep.

King's snoring gets worse. It sounds like a construction company is inside him, remodeling his skeleton. It keeps me up, so I decide to take a warm bath. Maybe that will help me fall asleep.

I take a magazine to read from the bedstand so I don't fall asleep in the tub. I'm notorious for falling asleep in tubs. Inside the bathroom, I kneel near the tub and start filling it up with warm water. While it's filling, I peek outside the open bathroom door to where King's black bag is propped up against the hotel room wall. I suppose he takes it with him wherever he goes, but I still have no idea what's inside it, minus the see-through money bag. I drape my arms over the side of the tub and splash my hands in the warm water as I mull over King's mysterious bag. I need to ask King what's in it. But forget the bag; I need to ask him to tell me more about himself. I know very little and being in a hotel room with him is plain stupid. My parents would have a heart attack if they knew.

Once the tub is three-quarters full, I hop in the warm water, close my eyes and gently lean my head back against the edge of the tub. Baths are heaven in water. The only thing missing is a bottle of bubbles.

Hearing a noise in the hotel room, I watch as the bathroom door creeps open. King peers in at me. "Honey! What are you doing?" he asks while staring down at me with astonished eyes.

"I'm taking a bath. Obviously."

He squats next to the tub and sticks his hand in the water. He pulls it back and declares, "What the hell! That's way too hot for your skin, honey. Hot water is horrible for your skin. That's why you have that skin fungus."

Shocked by his outburst, I slowly answer, "I can only take hot baths. I can't stand cold water. It kills me."

"It's awful for your skin. And you have bad skin."

I curl my legs to my chest and cross my arms in front. Sitting in the fetal position in the back of the tub, I stare at King. I feel like he just insulted me, or at least my skin, but I let it slide. Our relationship feels too new and worthless for arguments.

King removes the drain from the tub. I watch as the water swirls down the drain. My stomach twists in fear as I feel more and more exposed with the draining water. Then I look at King who is staring back at me. Oh God, he might kill me. This is it. This is how I'm going to die....

"Oh, man. I love how young you look right now. I love that about you. Okay, step out and dry off. I'll fill the tub again for you."

His voice is creepy. In it, I recognize some kind of mental pathology that makes every muscle fiber twitch with fear. I'm afraid to move, but I'm afraid to stay in the tub. Somehow, I slide my foot forward along the tub's slippery bottom and hoist myself up to a standing position. Shaking, I step out of the tub, grab a towel off the rack and dry myself. My subservient behavior shocks me. I'm never like this. I never follow orders from a man, but something about his voice casts a spell on me. I'm following his commands like a baby would its mother, as if in order to function at all, I need to be given commands. I feel like the only thing I can do right now is follow orders.

"Okay, honey," King whispers in a monotone voice. "Get in the tub now."

I drop the towel I'm clutching around my body, walk over to the tub and stick my right toe in the water. I quickly retract my foot, like I was just stung by a bee.

"No," I whimper. "It's way too cold."

"Get in the water, honey," King repeats. "It's good for you."

The combination of my nakedness, his size and harsh tone, and the fact that I don't know him that well or what he's hiding in his black bag keeps me from protesting further. I feel afraid of what might happen if I don't sit in the ice-cold tub water.

I put one foot in the water, followed by another and lower my body to the floor of the tub. My teeth start chattering in protest and a frantic, tapping noise fills my entire head. I hug my knees and start shivering uncontrollably while King stares down at me with a satisfied grin on his face. Goose bumps pop up all over my skin as my arm hair flies away from my body. Still, King stands in the bathroom grinning.

"This is too cold," I barely whisper.

"I know, honey. But it's good for you. Only cold water is good for your skin."

I grimace, but remain glued to the bottom of the tub.

"Damn, you look so young!" King says with a huge grin. "That's what I love about you. You look so young."

He leaves the bathroom as I sit shivering. I hear a bag rustle in the hotel room. Is he getting a knife? A gun? Oh God, Becka, stop shivering so you can defend yourself. You have to be able to move, I scold myself. The aroma of cold, spicy Thai food fills my nostrils. I can't tell if it makes my eyes water or if I'm crying. At least the rustling bag was the food. He must be eating.

I sit like an ice cube in the tub for ten minutes. Then ten minutes more. I hear the bed creek and King clears his throat. I hear him fiddling with the covers. Then silence.

It might be twenty minutes later. I've completely lost track of time. All the water in the tub has gone down the drain and left me behind, almost cruelly. I'm no longer shivering. Perhaps I'm in shock.

I grab the edge of the tub, step out and wrap myself in a towel. I look in the mirror, but quickly look away, down at the floor and exit the bathroom. King is snoring again, but I'm so exhausted, I don't care. I lower onto the opposite side of the bed, gently maneuver my body underneath the covers, close my eyes and go to sleep.

20

When I wake up, he's already gone. He sent a message to my phone telling me to meet him down at the workout spot. I yawn, get dressed in a t-shirt, shorts and sneakers, grab my inhaler and head to the beach.

It's a gorgeous day outside, sunny with a soothing breeze. A lot of early morning rollerbladers and bikers are out on the board walk. I spot King, wearing nothing but blue shorts, doing jumping jacks in the sand. He waves and I smile back.

"Just in time for the warm-up!" he cheerfully yells.

I jog over to him while he finishes another set of ten jumping jacks.

"You left early this morning," I comment.

"I know. Had to pick something up bright and early."

"For work?"

"Yeah."

"Oh," I say, while staring at the ocean. Suddenly, I'm filled with a desire to run along the shoreline and get my feet wet.

"Hey. I'm gonna run. And then I'll come back and join you for the rest of your workout," I tell King while lunging to the left to begin stretching.

"How far ya goin'?"

"About two miles," I answer. After lunging back and forth a bit, rolling both my ankles in a circular motion and stretching my arms, I hold my inhaler up to my mouth to take a puff. Before I do, King knocks it from my hand, causing me to skip backwards in surprise. I look at my inhaler, now in the sand, and then up at King.

"What are you doing?" I ask, both shocked and annoyed. "I need that!"

"That stuff is horrible for you," he says. "It only weakens your lungs and makes you dependent on something you don't need."

"I have asthma. I get asthma attacks! I need it," I say with authority. I bend down, pick up my inhaler and stubbornly puff it twice inside my mouth.

"Fine. Don't listen to me. But your lungs will never get better with that thing. You only think you need it. You need to do deep breathing exercises. That will get your lungs better," he says while taking a sip from a water bottle. I feel myself getting more and more annoyed, so I wave him away, turn toward the ocean and start jogging.

Immediately, I start to feel better. Running works like a quick mood booster for me, and I'm convinced it's nature's

Prozac. Plus, it works faster than all the antidepressants I've been on. I ran cross country in high school and was on the military school's marathon team, but lately, it's tougher and tougher to convince myself to go for a run, even though I know it'll make me feel better. Today, I'm excited to run. I'm sure running on a beautiful beach rather than the streets of Philadelphia has something to do with it.

I run about a mile and a half then turn around. Surprisingly, I'm moving fast. My anger and anxiety dissipate each time my foot hits the cool, moist, hard sand. By the time I get back to where I started, King's climbing up a thick rope with only his arms. The rope is between his outstretched muscular legs, and he isn't using them at all to propel himself up. I watch in awe as he makes it three quarters up the rope and comes back down. Damn, he's strong.

"How was your run?" he asks, a bit out of breath.

"Great. It beats running in Philly, that's for sure."

"And your breathing?" he asks, this time with sarcasm in his voice.

"Um, fine. Thanks to my inhaler," I snap back. I'm definitely pissed he knocked my inhaler in the sand earlier, and I probably would have made it an issue if it wasn't for the post-run endorphins filling my brain.

"Ready to do the rings?" he asks while jokingly punching my arm. Even that hurts.

"I'll give it a shot, but I don't like swinging things." I stare at the row of dangling rings while a guy who looks like a professional gymnast uses them. He gracefully swings from one ring to the other as if his alter ego is a monkey.

"Didn't you have to do this kind of stuff in a military school?" King asks while we walk over to the rings.

"Oh yeah. Lots of it," I answer and grimace just thinking back to all of my school's required ridiculous obstacle courses and physical fitness tests.

King goes first on the rings. He swings easily and smoothly from ring to ring with perfect timing. It looks like he's not even trying. I stand in the sand watching him go back and forth from ring to ring like a human pendulum. I'm getting hypnotized.

"Okay. Your turn, Becka," he announces after jumping from the last ring and softly landing in the sand.

"God," I mutter while wiping my sweaty hands against my shorts. "Okay, but this is not going to be pretty." I jump up and grab the first ring with my left hand. Just hanging there feels awkward. I start writhing my lower body in an attempt to gain some momentum. I glance at King who's standing with his arms folded across his chest and laughing at me.

"Want help?" he amusingly asks.

"Just a little," I holler back, sounding like I'm in pain.

He walks over and gently pushes my back. I move through the air and eye the next ring. My hands are sweating, and I feel my grasp getting weaker and weaker.

Awkwardly, I clasp the second ring and let go of the first. I lose my momentum and end up spinning in a really slow circle. Finally, after kicking my legs in the air, I gyrate haphazardly toward the third ring. I reach for it too early, right as my hand starts slipping from the second ring. For a moment, I'm suspended between the two rings and then, with a boom, I come crashing to the sandy ground below.

The first thing I hear is King's laugh. I look up but am blinded by the glare of the hot, morning sun. Then I feel his hand around mine and with little effort he pulls me up and onto my feet.

"You hurt?" he asks nonchalantly.

"No. Just sand in my eyes, I think," I answer while blinking my tearing eye rapidly back and forth.

"You'll get better. By the end of two weeks, you'll be able to do all of the rings. Maybe not both ways, but at least you'll get through them all," King encourages.

"In two weeks?" I ask while laughing. "That's the magic number, huh?"

"You'll see. You have to start out small and work up. You're out of shape right now. C'mon, let's do some bear crawls."

I follow King over to the tiny gravel track. He positions his body on all fours and begins slowly crawling around the perimeter. "C'mon! Let's go. This is the best exercise for your back. It will tighten you up quick," King yells while crawling.

I cringe. I'm hypersensitive about any comment that even remotely implies I'm overweight. I know I'm athletic, pretty, and guys like me, but I'm still perpetually insecure about my weight. Most people with eating disorders are, I suppose.

I get down on all fours and start crawling behind King. We crawl around the track once, and I'm sore. The exercise works my back muscles like I never experienced before. King starts on a second lap, so I follow. He's way ahead of me this time. I look up and notice a woman eying us curiously. She's thin, tan, and has her jet-black hair pulled back in a ponytail. As I'm about to crawl by her, she abruptly turns away, as if she's embarrassed. I smile and chuckle, while thinking King and I must look ridiculous. I must look like a wimpy polar bear attempting to keep up with a larger, fierce grizzly bear.

King completes three full laps of bear crawls. I do two and stretch during his third. Then he leads me through an abdominal session involving a variety of crunches, butterfly kicks, and planks. He follows that up with a series of pushups. Next, he works out his triceps on the horizontal bars, while I wimp out and ride on the swing. Finally, he motions me over to the pull-up bar. I watch as he easily pulls himself up and over the bar ten times in a row. His chest muscles proudly protrude outward, and his back muscles ripple with distinction. The man does not seem to tire.

"Okay, Becka. You're up. Knock 'em out!" King commands

in between breaths.

"Oh, God. I'll try. I can't do that many though," I say with wavering confidence. I stand under the bar, jump up and grab it. With great effort and audible grunting, I pull myself over the bar, though I'm pretty sure I'm cheating by sticking my chin up and out at the top. I lower myself to the point where my feet are almost touching the ground, then pull up again. The second pull-up is nowhere near as pretty as the first. I grunt so much on the second one that it sounds like I'm making love to the pull-up bar. After the second, I drop to the ground and wipe my hands on my shorts. "I'm done. That's it for today."

"You're done? C'mon, I thought you were tough!" King says as he grabs the pull-up bar again to do a quick set of seven. I watch in awe. Clearly, I'm not in shape compared to him.

"I used to do them, but I haven't practiced in a while," I offer.

"I know. I can tell. But that's what you're going to do while you're out here. You should be able to do five by the end of two weeks," King says after he finishes his set of seven.

"What is it with you and two weeks?" I teasingly ask again.

"Nothing. You'll just be a lot stronger by then. A different person. Especially with twice a day workouts!" King enthusiastically replies. It's like his energy never wanes.

"Twice a day? You do this twice a day? And you want me

to do it twice a day?"

"Yep. That's how you'll get fit. Trust me, baby," King says while stretching his arms.

"But we've been here for over two hours. It's almost lunch. When do you work?" I ask. I'm completely dumbfounded. It doesn't seem like he has time for work given his exercise regime.

"I told you. I have my own hours. I'm only doing pro bono now. Don't need the money and don't want it," he says.

"Oh, okay, whatever. Anyhow, I'm actually starving. Do you want to eat something?" My stomach is growling up a storm.

"Yes. We can get something to eat on Third Street. I'm gonna take a dip in the ocean though first. You want to come?"

"Nah, I'm good," I say. The water is way too cold for me.

King jogs over to the ocean and wades out until he has to tread water. As I watch him gracefully move his arms through the water like knives through melted butter, the curious woman who observed us earlier taps me on my shoulder from behind.

"That man has an amazing presence. What a beautiful man," she says.

"Thank you," I respond to her. I sound as if someone complimented me on my dog. She must think I'm being aggressive, because she nervously giggles and quickly jogs away, as if I'm a woman decisively marking my territory. I shrug. Nothing could be further from the truth.

21

King and I walk side by side to the Promenade on Third Street. It's bubbling with beautiful, fit people in trendy clothes. They are lustfully gawking in the windows of ritzy stores and looking to buy more things. I see a sports store and ask King if we can go inside. I want to look for a sweatshirt. He shrugs as if he doesn't care and follows me in the store. A pretty, petite Asian girl in a halter top and short skirt comes in after us. King smiles at her and says hello.

"Do you know her?" I ask.

"Just being friendly," he says and begins perusing the display of running shoes. I buy a sweatshirt and walk back outside with King. As we walk, he says, "You know that Asian girl didn't have any panties on."

"What?" I stop walking and glare at him. I'm both shocked and disgusted.

"She wasn't…"

"Yeah, well, okay, but… why were you looking there? That's gross," I declare shifting farther away from him on the sidewalk.

"I notice everything like that," King says with a pompous chuckle.

"Disturbing," I snap.

I spot a deli and tell King I'm going inside to order a sandwich. He tells me he'll wait outside. After ordering and paying for a turkey sub, I sit down at an outdoor table. My stomach sounds like a motorboat garage so I dig in. King's workout certainly upped my appetite.

While eating, I look around for King, finally spotting him standing next to an outdoor newspaper stand. He looks like he's anxiously waiting for something. I holler his name between swallows and he finally waves, holding up his index finger. Then he grabs a paper off the rack and hustles over to my table.

"So, what did you get?" he asks after sitting down.

"A turkey sub," I remark quickly. "Hey… did you not pay for that paper for some reason? I think you're supposed to pay in the store."

King doesn't answer. Instead he opens up the paper and starts reading. That really annoys me so I ask again with more force, "King! How come you didn't pay for the paper?"

"Becka, seriously! Would you relax! It's a stupid paper," he yells while violently flipping through some pages. I determine he's flipping too fast to actually be reading any of the articles.

"So you did just steal a newspaper!" I accuse him while slapping my hand on the table. "Why on earth would you steal that? You don't have a dollar? And you're a lawyer, supposed to be all about the law."

"It's just a paper. Heck, I can put it back once I'm done reading it if that makes you feel better?"

"No. I don't really care." Truthfully, I don't care whether he stole the paper or not. I think King's behavior is bizarre, but at the same time, the image of him swiping a newspaper humors me. He seems to greatly enjoy the paper too, as he completely tunes me out to read it. I shrug and begin people watching.

"You know, Becka. I usually either do work or read the paper during this time," he finally says. "You should start carrying your medical books with you so you can do the same. You need to start studying, honey."

I sigh. For a minute, I contemplate telling him the truth: that I just quit school and really have no future plans. Instead I nod in agreement. I did pack two of my books, maybe because part of me is in denial about willingly walking away from a prestigious medical degree, or because I don't have an identity outside of med school. Oh well, a little extra knowledge never killed anyone.

Then I strategically change the subject. "Why haven't you eaten anything? I feel obese after demolishing this sandwich in front of you," I comment.

"Because I already ate."

"Where?" I innocently ask.

He forcefully drops the newspaper to the table and says, "Becka, you ask way too many questions. That's the one thing that annoys me. I'm fine. I'm not hungry. I ate this morning."

"Geez, no need to get all upset. I was just asking." I figure that, with the way he works out, he'd be hungry all the time.

After two hours of more people watching and small chitchat, we head back down to the beach for King's second workout of the day. The day is still hot with a little less sun than the morning. After putting his bags down, he jumps up toward the clear, blue sky, crouches back down, and mumbles words in between. It looks like he's chanting.

"What was that?" I ask when he looks finished.

"Praying. Now going to jump in the ocean. Want to come?"

"No. I'm good," I emphatically state.

King laughs. "Wow. You really hate cold water, don't you?"

"Ya think?"

After diving through some waves and a short swim, he shakes off and then climbs the rope again—twice. Then he does another set of bear crawls. Next, the horizontal bars followed by more swinging rings. I jump in here and there, but mostly I stretch on a tiny piece of grass and ride on a playground's swing while admiring his incredible display of strength. My arms are too sore from the morning's workout for much else. I decide to bring a soccer ball to the beach so I can play while King works out. At least that'll save me from a second rigorous arm workout.

By the time he's done, the sun is setting. Brilliant colors splatter across the sky in mysterious patterns. Pinks, blues, whites and yellows. I breathe it all in and decide if I can see a sky like that every day, life would be more tolerable.

As we start walking back to the hotel, I buy a bottle of water from the bike rental place. Two friendly Mexican guys are working the stand. We say hello and talk for a bit until one of them points at King and asks, "Are you with him?"

I take a swig from the bottled water and nod. The two Mexicans' postures stiffen. They look at each other as if they share a dark secret. I study their faces for clues but can't decipher their unspoken messages. I want to ask, but one of them relaxes and says, "He's an okay guy. He's not a bad guy."

I hesitantly nod, though still confused, turn and walk back to King. We start walking back to the hotel together while joking along the way. At the hotel door I ask, "So do you need to go home for anything?"

"No. In the morning, I'll have to make a quick run back, but I'll do that before you get up," he says.

"Not even a change of clothes?" I ask.

"No, honey. I'll get what I need in the morning. Unless you want me to go home?"

"No. I just thought you might have to. I still want to see

where you live though!" I chime back.

"You want to go right now?"

"No, the hotel's right here and I'm exhausted."

"Ha! You're weak! When your stay is up here, I'll take you to my crib," King promises.

Right after entering the hotel room, I do a belly flop on the closest, queen-size bed and instantly close my eyes. My limbs are done, and I know I won't be getting up for the rest of the night. King hops in the other bed, which is fine by me. I'm too tired to cuddle and for anything else.

Before I drift into a deep sleep, I glance over at him. He's propped up in bed reading the Bible. I chuckle, slam my head back down on the bed and pass out.

22

It's morning, 5:30 AM, and I'm up as early as King. I clear a space at the hotel desk and read aloud from my pathology book. King insists I do it, since he's worried I'm falling behind in studies I don't have any more.

"Read it out loud again. That will help it sink in," King commands from his comfortable position on the bed.

I read a paragraph on leukemia and lymphomas out loud while King listens intently. When I'm finished, he gets out of bed and walks to the bathroom.

"Can I stop now? I want to get breakfast. Aren't you bored yet listening to all of this?" I holler from my desk chair.

"You have to do this, honey. You don't want to slack in your studies. And no, I'm not bored. I love medicine. I read it for leisure. I may go back to medical school, actually," he yells back.

"Why? You're already a lawyer, Overachiever. You'd be an old student. How old are you, anyhow?"

"Thirty-nine," he says while coming out of the bathroom. "What about you?"

"Wow. I didn't think you were that old. I'm twenty-five."

"Darn it. I didn't think you were that old," he says while jokingly swatting my arm. I laugh too.

"Does our age difference bother you at all?" I ask.

"Honey, please. I've had women younger than you. Men age better than women. It's just a fact. Most women my age don't look as good," he says while rubbing lotion on his body.

"Yeah. I guess. Though I've seen some really pretty older women. It sucks to be female in our society and grow old," I say while closing my pathology book.

"Yep. You guys have a short shelf life," he says nonchalantly. "Okay. I'll meet you at our spot later. I have to run an errand."

"Where to?" I ask, still stinging from his remark.

"Have to stop by the court room to pick up some papers."

"Oh. Okay."

"But first," he says while wrapping his massive arms around my shoulders and kissing my cheek. "I want to have you."

My lips meet his for a brief second. Then he scoops me up and out of the chair and gently places me on the bed.

"King," I whisper while looking in his eyes. "Please be gentle this time. I'm really sore from our workout."

"Shh, baby. I will," he says then closes his eyes. I close my eyes too and look away. It feels better than the last couple of times, but still not one hundred percent right. Something is still way off. Something is still forced. It feels like I'm here, but I'm not.

A few hours later, I'm at the workout spot, kicking the soccer ball around in the sand. It's warm and cheerful out. I'm dribbling back and forth on the square of green grass and juggling the ball with my thighs and feet. Soccer always improves my mood. It makes me feel like I'm dancing, and the ball is my patient partner. I feel good, except for my stomach. My stomach feels nauseous, most likely due to the birth control pill I swallowed earlier. I didn't mention anything to King, but I brought a box of contraceptives with me that I picked up at a Savannah pharmacy, and I took my first one this morning. The last thing I want is to get pregnant. God knows I'm not in my right frame of mind and getting pregnant would only make my life more hell. A side effect of the pill is abdominal discomfort, which is also a side effect of the antidepressant I'm taking. There's basically zero chance I won't feel like vomiting.

King arrives an hour later as I'm attempting to properly rub sun block on my arms and neck. I'm starting to burn and look more like a beet every second.

"Hey there!" I say with a smile. "Can you help rub this lotion on me? I'm burning up, and melanoma runs in my family."

"Not now. I have to jump in the water. Later," he grumbles. His gait is angry.

"Can you just do my back? It'll take two seconds!" I argue.

"No, honey. Please! I just told you that I need to jump in

the water! I'm burning up," he snaps.

Before I can respond, he's already jogging toward the ocean. I watch as he submerges below the water, resurfaces, gets out and runs back over to me.

"What was that all about?" I ask as he forcefully grabs the sun block from my hands and vigorously rubs it on my back.

"Nothing. I just have my routine and like to stick to it."

"Well, you didn't have to snap. Did you have a bad day at court or something?" I ask.

"No. I always do good. I wage war in the court room, honey. You know this. And I didn't have a case today. I just had to pick up papers."

"Okay. So, I was thinking of going swimming."

"In the ocean? Finally!" he remarks with amusement.

"No, no, someone at the hotel told me there's a YMCA in Santa Monica that has a pool. I'm going to swim there. I need to keep track of the laps I swim," I say.

"Oh. Okay, okay. You going now?"

"Yeah. Where should I meet you later?"

"Did you bring your med books with you this time?" he asks.

Damn, he won't give that up. "I did, yes. Want me to come by your office?"

"Hmm, not today. Meet me at the library. Do you know where that is?"

"Yep. Hey, do you want to grab a drink tonight? I'm not

a big drinker, but I feel like I could use one," I say.

"If you want. Whatever. But I'm still working out tonight. Twice a day, that's what I do."

"Don't I know it!" I say and laugh. "Okay, I'll meet you at the library."

I start walking away from the beach, but catch sight of King's brown grocery bag. At first I think it is the same bag he always carries, but this one looks cleaner. He must have exchanged bags.

"King!" I call back. "What is in your bag? Did you get a new one?"

"It's my food! Yes, the other one was falling apart. You ask too many questions!" he says. Then he drops on the ground and starts doing push-ups.

"No I don't. I was just wondering what kind of food is in there."

"Nothing you'd like. Go swim. You're wasting valuable workout time, and I thought you wanted to get in shape."

I roll my eyes at him, turn and walk up the hilly street toward the YMCA.

After swimming a relaxing mile, I shower, dry off, and walk a few short blocks lined with bright tiny houses to the library. My post-exercise endorphins keep me temporarily high and content. While walking, King sends a text message telling me he's on the second floor of the library reviewing his notes. Whatever that means.

23

I spot his massive frame hunched over a yellow notebook and a laptop computer on one of the library's large oak tables. I guess he carries his laptop around in the black bag. One mystery solved.

There are a few disheveled folks in odd outfits, like heavy winter coats with flipflops and baseball caps, sitting at the table over from King's, but aside from that, the library appears empty. I quietly walk over to King's table and take a seat.

"Hey," I whisper.

"Hey. Did you bring your book with you?" he whispers back.

"Yep," I say while glancing at the adjacent table. "There are a lot of homeless people in here."

"Yep," King answers dismissively and looks back down at his notebook.

"What are you doing?" I ask again, obviously trying to find any distraction to keep me from pretend-studying material I absolutely hate.

"I'm working on financial issues for my father's estate in Nigeria," he quietly answers.

I nod and strain my neck to see what he's writing in the notebook. It looks like a bunch of scribbles, numbers and random lists. I can't make sense of it. I shrug, figuring I should quit prying and let him do his work. I look back down at my open medical book and attempt to read the first paragraph. None of the words make sense, so I stop and stare at the adjacent homeless people instead. All of them are slumped over newspapers with their eyes closed. Not one of them is actually reading the paper. I chuckle out loud but quickly cover my mouth. I can't help it. The scene reminds me of something I used to do in the army during field training. When out in the woods for hours at a time and told to "secure the perimeter," my buddies and I would balance the tips of our helmets on our rifles to make it appear we were on the look-out. In reality, our eyes were closed and we were napping.

I'm able to refocus and skim through my medical book for about an hour. As always, the diseases come alive and taunt me with thoughts of death and dying. I slam my pathology book closed and start reading a section on ethics in my medical philosophy book. Of course, I can't even do that. My tolerance for all things medical is a dead horse. Pushing the books aside, I lean back in my chair and silently berate myself. This is easy and you're smart, I think to myself. The idea that I don't want it is unacceptable. That doesn't count. My own wishes never do. I never choose to do the things I like. I might as well be a mannequin the world dresses as it sees fit. I bite the inside of my right cheek and feel my eyes well up with tears. I feel like a quitter, a complete failure. I close my eyes and try to nap and probably look like just another homeless person pretend-reading.

"Becka... Becka!" someone whispers loudly. "Wake up!"

I lift my head off the table and blink furiously as my eyes adjust to the light. I rub my hand across the table. It's wet. I look down. I drooled all over it.

"Sorry! I must have fallen asleep."

"I noticed. Are you ready for workout session number two? I'm heading to the spot now."

"Huh? Already? Oh... okay. Sure. I'm ready."

I'm carrying a black backpack filled with my soccer ball, bathing suit, and medical books. King is carrying the usual black knapsack and brown paper bag. We walk silently from the library to the workout spot.

"Somethin' bothering you?" King asks.

"Nope. I'm good," I answer. Another lie. I'm far from good. I pretty much have no idea who I am or what I'm doing anymore. All I know is that I'm working out like a crazy woman, but working out with King is surprisingly fun and calming. King. I have no idea who he really is or why he's suddenly the center of my life. I feel like I've entered an alternative universe, a Manic Kingdom, like I've fallen down the rabbit hole...but "I'm good."

King leads me through another rigorous workout session at the beach. This time, I really try to keep up. He's more encouraging and tells me I already look better than yesterday. I even make it to the fourth swinging ring without falling. I do crunches, push-ups and finish with three laps of bear crawls. Then I collapse on the bench to rest, while he jumps in the ocean and says a prayer. When he's finished with his routine, I suggest we grab a drink at an Irish pub along Ocean Ave. I don't even know why I want a drink, but I do. He doesn't seem excited over the idea, but reluctantly agrees. He puts on a long-sleeved white shirt and asks if it's okay to wear that. After all, it's all he's got.

"Yeah, of course. I don't care what you wear." I never care what people wear.

We walk to the cute Irish pub I saw earlier and sit at the bar. The only other people in the bar are a group of rowdy drunk men and the bartenders. I ask King what he wants, but he shakes his head back and forth.

"Nothing?" I ask, alarmed. "Not even water?"

"Just water," he says while folding his arms across

his chest. He stares straight above the bar at a TV screen featuring a football game. He looks uncomfortable.

I order a Long Island Iced Tea, and end up drinking it way too fast. Feeling buzzed and extra friendly, I pull at King's still-crossed arm, but he shakes me away. I shrug, walk over to the jukebox, put in a dollar, and start picking out songs. Suddenly, Poison blares from the box, and I start dancing. One of the rowdy drunk men smiles at me and comes over. He looks like a has-been, striped-shirt frat boy with too much gel in his hair. He's completely not my type, but I guess I'm his. He puts his arm around my waist and starts swaying back and forth with me.

King, who's still sitting at the bar, turns around and notices. His eyes narrow, and he looks irate. I smile at him, to let him know I'm perfectly okay and having fun. My reassurance doesn't seem to matter. King gets up so fast that his bar stool falls over sideways and hits the floor with a thud. He struts over to me and says, "Let's go. Now."

"What? Why? I'm fine! I'm just having fun," I say in a tipsy tone. I'm buzzing, but I'm not drunk, and I really want to stay and dance.

"C'mon dude," the drunk man stutters. "She's just having fun."

"Stay the hell out of this!" King snaps and shoots the man a fierce glance. The man, who's sarcastically grinning at King, isn't anywhere near King's size. King would crush him in a fight with one blow. I know I have to keep that from happening.

"Okay, okay. King! Let's just go. Okay?" I say to King while grabbing his arm.

He and the drunk guy are still glaring at each other, like two feral street cats ready to fight. I pray no one swings, but King looks like he's up for a war. While still eying the drunk guy, King swiftly turns around and walks with me to the door. His gait is pressured, as if it's taking all of his will power to walk away from the fight.

Once outside, walking briskly in the chilly night toward our hotel, I ask him, "What the hell was that all about? He was harmless!"

"Becka, please. You didn't see the way that punk was looking at you. I did you a favor," he responds angrily.

"Well at least he talked to me! You sat there all night like someone pissed in your beer! No, water! You didn't even drink!" I shoot back.

"God, you're so annoying buzzed. Let's just walk, please? I have a busy day tomorrow. I don't want to listen to this abuse."

"Abuse? I'm just talking!" I say in disbelief.

"No, it's abuse."

"What the...? Are you on drugs? I'm just asking you a question. I was having fun and you went ahead and started a fight! Abuse? Are you crazy?"

"I'm not going to listen to this anymore. Let's just walk. I'm tired."

"No, I want to settle this!"

"I don't. You're drunk. Just shut up, will you? Just shut up!"

"Why are you being so mean to me? You're the one who caused all the drama tonight! This is all your fault!" I yell.

Before I can say anything else, King pushes me away. It's a light push, but I stumble and grab on to a light post to steady myself. I feel my ears starting to burn as tears fill my eyes. Afraid of crying, I decide not to say anything else. That was a light push. My gut tells me the next one could be a serious blow.

From there, we walk in silence back to the hotel room. Silently, I change into my pajamas while King uses the bathroom and crawls into bed. Still peeved, I crawl into the other bed, though I can't fall asleep. I'm scared. I'm buzzed. I'm upset. I want to talk, but I don't want to talk. I want to be held, but I don't know by who.

My eyes are closed when I feel King's warm arm around my waist and the mattress shake as he climbs into bed with me.

"I'm sorry," he whispers in my ear. He falls asleep instantly. The annoying snoring starts. I lie awake, motionless, still wondering who it is I want to hold me.

24

The next morning, I can't get out of bed. I'm somewhere between dreaming and waking, that place where confusion controls everything. My eyes blink back and forth before finally opening. I sluggishly roll to my side and feel stiff all over. I squint at the light beaming underneath the hotel window curtains. It's morning. I have to check out of the hotel, and I'm concerned. Is my depression back with a vengeance? Am I glued to my bed again?

I wiggle my toes and feel aches in my calves and thighs. As my mind becomes more conscious, I realize my soreness is muscular in nature. I sigh with relief. My pain is a direct result of King's insane workout regime, and that's a good thing. I'll take muscle soreness over the crippling rigidity that always accompanies depression any day.

I hop out of bed and wince. The backs of my calves are burning. Pain explodes like a grenade across my lower back. Slowly, I begin stretching. It's going to be a long day, and I have to pack and check out of the hotel. Tonight will be my first night at King's place, and I can't wait to see it.

"King," I whimper. "I am so sore."

King steps out of the bathroom and looks at me. He's wearing his token blue shorts and rubbing lotion all over his body, which I noticed is part of his morning hygienic routine. "That's good, baby! You're getting back in shape. My workout is the best there is. You'll see."

"I might feel that way when I can walk again," I complain while hobbling over to my suitcase to pick out a pair of shorts and t-shirt to wear. "By the way, do you ever wash your shorts?"

"I did last night. Soap and water in the sink. You want to smell them?" he jokes. "By the way, you really need to start lubricating your skin every day. Look at my skin. I have the best skin, and I'm fourteen years older than you! Women want me, because the first thing they see is my skin. Don't be lazy. Lazy people don't get anywhere. And lubricate everything. Your face, your toes, even the bottom of your feet. Twice a day. That's how often you should lubricate. Trust me."

"I would if I could lift my arms!" I yell back. "Fine. Toss me the bottle when you're done."

"When you're done, head down to our spot. I'll meet you there in a few hours. I gotta go to the courthouse today," he says.

I nod while yawning. I plan on sleeping for another

hour or two before heading to the workout spot. King can call me lazy. I don't care.

A few hours and two coffees later, I meet King at our spot. He's already climbing the ropes. It's a breezy, cloudless, humidity-free day. Perfect weather for an asthmatic to work out. Our spot isn't crowded, which is even better. I think it's cute that King refers to the outdoor gym area as "our spot." Of course it isn't our spot, but I guess we spend so much time here that it might as well be.

I'm still sore and sluggish, so I mope in a free swing and watch an elderly man, dressed only in black shorts and sneakers, ride a mountain bike around the gravel track. His thin grey hair and wrinkled, sun-spotted skin puts him at about seventy-five, but his shaped body can pass for a forty-year-old. I've seen him on his bike before, but I never bothered to talk to him.

Suddenly, he stops riding, puts his bike down gently in the sand, and sits on the freshly cut lawn. I hop up and out of my swing and plop down next to him. Inhaling the pleasant smell of trimmed grass, I smile at him. He smiles back at me.

"Nice day, isn't it?" I say while gazing up at the sky.

The old man is panting for air while alternating between drinking his water bottle and pouring it over his head. I feel intrusive and am about to get up and leave when he says, "Hi."

I smile again. "Hi! Do you live around here?"

He takes another swig from his water bottle and is panting less. He points to a building in the distance and says, "I'm a caretaker. For that apartment complex over there. I've lived here for years."

"You're lucky! What a great place to live."

He points to King, who's still climbing the rope, and asks, "Are you with him?"

I smile sheepishly and say, "I guess so. I guess we are together. It all happened really fast."

He giggles, slaps his thigh and says, "You don't sound so sure of yourself!"

"I'm definitely not sure of anything," I laugh.

I continue to giggle as the old man stands up, bends over and touches his toes. I watch him stretch and realize how comfortable and natural I feel sitting next to him. I enjoy being around lively, fit, elderly people, but the ones burdened with health issues and confined to hospital beds always frighten and depress me. They are visible reminders of how I'll ultimately become, and it makes me anxious. When I worked as a med student on the hospital floors, the bed-bound, debilitated, senile patients always made me feel like taking off my white coat, sprinting out the hospital door, and engaging in wild times that involved buckets of alcohol and dancing. I felt like I wanted to run away from life or at least die young. The circle of life is ruthless.

"Do you know him?" I ask while nodding toward King.

The old man chuckles and says, "I've seen him around. I mean, he's always here."

"I know," I remark. "It's almost as if he doesn't do anything else but work out, right?"

"Yep. Do you love him?" he asks. I'm taken aback.

"Love him?" I ask while partially grimacing and looking at King. "Oh. No, no, no, no. He's nice. I like hanging out with him. I like working out with him. Love? God, no. I mean, I seriously just met him."

"You can fall in love in seconds. Are you one of those jaded girls?" he asks with a sarcastic look in his eyes. He studies me some more. "You look to be about the jaded age."

"Umm. No…I don't think so. I just don't fall in love that fast."

"Good. You shouldn't. If you do it too fast, you'll end up with the wrong person and be looking for a way out when the love dries up."

"Yeah. That would suck," I agree.

The old man laughs and drinks some more water while I dig the dirt from my finger nails and think about all the people in the world who fall in love too fast. I know so many. Love is like a drug that way. People want it so badly, they'll pretend something that isn't it is it.

"You know," the old man starts while interrupting me from my thoughts and nails. "It's better to be alone than wish you were."

His words strike me like a blow to the face that locks them inside my head. I'm not sure what he means, but my body perks up and responds in a way only words full of wisdom can move a body. It's that kind of mysterious wisdom that creates adrenaline now but reveals itself later. I don't feel like he's giving me general advice. I feel like he's giving me a hint. His voice sounds downright ominous.

"What?" I say, a little off guard.

He nods his head slightly toward the direction of King, winks and quietly whispers, "You heard me."

He grabs his bike from the ground, hops on it, waves and rides away. I sit in the grass, while goose bumps colonize my skin. I feel uneasy and glance over at King, who's now doing bear crawls. I stare at him and decide he reminds me of a cartoon, because he wears the same blue swim trunks and carries the same possessions every day.

King stops crawling, stands up and jogs over to me. "Hey! What's up? Why aren't you working out? And why were you talking to that crazy old man? He's senile!"

"I like him. He's a cute, vibrant old man. I like that," I respond absentmindedly.

"Well, he's crazy," King quickly states. "Don't listen to a word he says."

I glance confusingly at King but decide to change the subject. I don't know if the old man's words spooked me or if I'm just feeling brave, but I need to know more about King this very instant, even though I know my questions annoy the hell out of him.

"So, are you really a lawyer?" I ask, trying to sound as innocent as possible.

"Yes I am," King responds as he stretches out his arms. "Is another round of questions coming?"

"No," I say with a little chuckle. Maybe I am annoying, but as far as I'm concerned he could be anything. "Do you think you can show me your legal office one day? Or introduce me to your friends? I mean, I'm with you, and I feel like I don't know much about you or your life in Nigeria. You lived there first, right?"

King tenses up and seems disturbed. He begins pacing back and forth, which makes me think of Chase pacing in my apartment. It's the first time I really think of Chase before quitting my life in Philadelphia, and it makes me queasy.

"I hope you didn't listen to that old man, honey," King angrily shouts. "He's crazy! In due time, I'll show you everything. Relax! What are you so nervous about? I don't wear all of my armor to show the world. I'm a private person. You want to know about my life in Nigeria? My family was rich, real rich. I had a gorgeous pad and ten acres all to myself! My mother was a beautiful African queen, stunning, better than any white girl I've ever seen, but she cheated on my father, a brilliant, great man. I loved my daddy. Still do. Amazing man. Did I tell you he was a Fulbright scholar? Do you know how difficult that is? He ended up taking me to America and never allowed my mother to see me again. He wasn't one to mess with, I'll tell you that. That was how he punished her for cheating on him. She wasn't allowed to see her baby ever again, but you know, she brought it on herself. After a while, my father married a white Irish gal, just like you, in New York City."

"That's so sad," I quietly whisper. "It's so sad you never got to see your real mother again."

"She did it to herself. It is what it is," King says.

We are both quiet while listening to the musical arrangement of oceanic noises. Then I ask, "So you went to law school at NYU and came out here to practice?

"Yep," King says while stretching his legs and sighing. "I came out here and made it big. Won every case. Now I'm just livin' the dream, because I can."

"Okay," I say, unconvinced. None of this makes any sense. Everything feels like it will crumble right in front of my eyes one day.

"Alright. Enough of the questions. It's getting late. I'm going to jump in the ocean and cool off," King barks as he turns and jogs toward the ocean.

King's subduing tale makes me want to remain stationary on the sand, but I force myself to hop on my feet and walk toward the shoreline. By the time I get there, King's already slamming into waves. I watch as the foamy, grey water breaks against his chocolate skin. He has such an uncanny relationship with the ocean. In an earlier conversation, he told me that he absolutely needed to go into the ocean four times a day. It seems like every time we argue or he grows irritated, he insists on jumping in the water. Afterward, when he's back on shore and drying off with a towel, he's always happier and forgiving. It's as if the cool ocean absorbs the heat from his aggressive furnace for a brain.

Still swimming, he looks over at me, smiles and motions me to join him in the water. I shake my head back and forth to indicate I won't. I'm a great swimmer and life guard qualified, but a weary sensation in my gut keeps me anchored on the sand.

There's something phony about the way he gestures me with his hand. Like our love making, it seems like something is missing. He looks so confident and effortlessly buoyant that each time he beckons me into the ocean, I feel like I'm being challenged by a formidable sea creature who's master of his liquid domain. As many times as I've ignored my gut, I listen to it when it comes to going in the water with King. I will not go in the water.

25

That night, King and I randomly decide to have a picnic in the sand, under the stars. While King chants his painfully long nightly prayers, I walk to a snack shop off the boardwalk and purchase two sandwiches, waters and a bag of pretzels. He's already sitting Indian style in the sand by the time I get back. The sun is setting over the ocean and the breeze picks up, so I put on a sweatshirt to stay warm.

"Is it good?" I ask as he takes a first bite of his sandwich.

"Yep. But not as good as my stuff." He wipes his mouth with one hand while holding the brown bag up with the other.

"Well, what is in there?" I ask with overflowing curiosity. "You never told me, and you never share."

"'Cause if you like it too much, there won't be any left for me," he says and chuckles. "Hurry up and finish, honey. We have a long way to walk yet. My house is near the canals."

I nod and bite into my turkey sandwich. The rich taste of sliced turkey, Swiss cheese and mayonnaise temporarily distracts me from wondering about the mysterious contents in King's brown bag. While chewing, I look around the beach. It's practically desolate. There's a few misfits still around. A deranged street lady with untamed hazel eyes is shouting obscenities and throwing punches at a homeless man who appears to be warding her off from his life's treasures, a shopping cart full of empty crushed aluminum cans. I saw both of them embracing and kissing each other by the public bathroom earlier this week. I guess they have a volatile relationship. I chuckle and say out loud, "Well, at least they'll never have the problem of figuring out whose house to stay over each night."

King doesn't say anything. He's staring out at the ocean and ignoring me. I look around the beach area and notice more homeless people with lethargic postures parked on blankets or benches. Like a nocturnal bug invasion, they seem to come from nowhere and multiply in numbers as night nears. I often see them huddled together, laughing, talking and passing around a bottle or two. I guess they benefit from each other's company and body warmth. I wonder what I would do if I were homeless. I'd want to be delusional and pretend I weren't homeless – like a weathered smelly lady with Einstein hair and mad eyes who tells everyone she's a princess. I'd also want to be homeless in the country because everything is friendlier than in a city. I might steal berries or corn and raid garbage cans during the day. At night I'd sneak into a quiet barn, maybe with an animal or two to ward off loneliness, and sleep soundly in a thick bed of soft hay.

"You ready to go, honey?" King impatiently asks. "It's getting late, and you are daydreaming again. And you need to study your medical books. I want you to read a chapter to me out loud every night. That way, we'll both learn. Okay? More, more, more!"

"I'm ready," I chirp while jumping to my feet and wiping the sand off my clothes. "Boy, there are a lot of homeless people here," I randomly announce.

"Helpless," King emphatically states. "They are helpless. There's a difference between being homeless and helpless."

I laugh. "Whatever you say. But they don't look like they have homes."

King instantly looks agitated. He pushes himself off the ground and says, "Okay. Let's go. You need to walk more too. You need to be tighter. Your body needs to be tighter. You are a little loose under your chin. I want you to be tighter like the girls out here. Walking will do that for you."

I don't respond to King's slight insult about my figure, although it does get me to forget about the homeless people and start walking. Despite my desperate mind, I intuitively know he's purposely making me feel insecure, though why he wants to, I'm not sure yet. Maybe it's his way of getting me in the best shape of my life. I don't know. Still, I'm aware that great manipulators use one's insecurities as steering wheels to drive that person in any direction they please. And if I didn't need him as a lifeline, I'd probably fight with him or, at least, put my guard up more.

After picking up my bag at the hotel front desk, we walk on the sidewalk toward Venice, passing vibrant, trendy bars and restaurants as we go. I always look inside when we pass them, but King doesn't seem interested. Based on his reaction the first time we went to a bar together, I figure he wants nothing to do with them. He's antisocial, but I'm okay with that. At the moment, I only want to be with him.

"Hey," King says and turns back to look at me. My nosiness for the bar scene has caused me to fall behind. "What do they call the songs soldiers sing?"

"Cadences. We sang them a lot," I call back.

"Cadences, nice. Sometimes I sing them on my walk between home and the workout spot. The Africans used to sing them, too. While picking cotton in the fields," he says.

I nod in agreement while picturing hundreds of estranged Africans singing cadences while picking cotton. It makes me sad. King says something else about cotton and Africans, but I don't respond. He's black. I'm white with a million guilt complexes. It's best to avoid any sort of slavery talk.

We continue walking but with each step my bag feels heavier and heavier. I start to take frequent breaks by dropping my bag for three seconds, stretching out my arms, picking it up and starting again. It feels like we've already walked two miles. "King," I finally say. "Are we almost there?"

"Yep. Almost," he answers without looking back.

"I wish we took a cab or something." I say, even though from the looks of things, there are no cabs in LA. I feel like I'm back on a road-march. "My bag is so heavy and awkward," I whine.

King stops in his tracks, turns around, and walks toward me. He gently removes the bag strap off my throbbing shoulder. He puts it over his left shoulder, while still carrying both his grocery bag and black laptop case. Then he turns back around and starts walking again. "Thank you," I say with a shrug. All I'm left to carry is my backpack and myself.

We walk about another mile before King stops in front of a large, modern white house with a "For Sale" sign out front. I drop my bag on the sidewalk in front of the house and start guzzling from my water bottle. My mouth and throat both feel hot and dry. I'm hot all over, really. Even though it's breezy and I'm lightly dressed in a sweatshirt and shorts, I'm still sweating.

"Wait here. I have to check something," King says to me.

I nod as King quietly goes around the back of the house. Two minutes later, he opens the front door and gestures me to come inside. Once inside, I drop my backpack in a large, empty, bright white room. I slowly walk around the spotless downstairs and glance around from top to bottom.

I'm absolutely stunned. The entire house is empty. The only object in the house is a plastic, water bottle on the kitchen counter. King picks it up and starts drinking from it. All I can do is stare at him with an open mouth.

"King," I apprehensively start while still looking around the house. "Your entire house is empty. What the hell? Are we trespassing? Are we going to get arrested?"

"Shh, Becka. Keep your voice down. Do you want to wake the neighbors? I told you my things are in storage. I'm in between houses so there's no point for me to put everything in this one, only to have to move it again."

"This is absurd. There's nothing," I comment while still taking in the vast emptiness of his place. My heart rate quickens as I question if I am trespassing in a strange house with a strange man. I want to sprint back to a comfortable, furnished, safe hotel room, but I can't. I'm low on cash and exhausted.

"I don't need a lot of things. We've been through this," King assures me while leaning against the large island in the middle of the kitchen.

"I know. But, I mean… nothing? Are you Buddhist or something?" I ask, half-jokingly, half-not. Maybe he is eccentric. My mom once told me I have a great uncle who ditched society to live in a shack deep in the woods with ten cats. Eccentrics are out there.

"No, honey. Becka, why do you say such stupid things? I

told you, my things are in storage. Are you one of those girls who needs to see her man's wealth to get happy? Sometimes I wonder," he frustratingly responds.

"What?" I ask incredulously while taking a step back from him. "Are you serious? I don't care about material stuff at all! It's just that your house is empty, and I'm not used to that."

My parents always taught me to value people over things, and I do. I'm also depressed and severely apathetic, meaning I'm even less materialistic than my baseline. Material things couldn't cure my depression, so I care zilch about what a person owned or didn't own. Especially King. It's pathetic, but he's the only person who gives me a reason to get out of bed in the morning. I know, with all my heart, that I have to hold on to him.

"I'm tired. One day, I'll show you everything I own. Then maybe you'll be impressed," King says, both bitterly and softly.

"King. I don't care. Seriously. I don't. It just shocked me, is all. I'm also tired and have to go to the bathroom. My head hurts and I'm not thinking straight. Where's the bathroom?" I ask while glancing around.

"There's one right here," he says while pointing to a thin, wooden door off of the kitchen. "And one upstairs. But there's no toilet paper."

"No toilet paper? But I have to…um…go." I explain with

a sense of urgency.

"Then after you go, flush, and when the bowl refills, scoop a little of the water up with your hand, and wash yourself that way. The water is clean and actually healthier for you than sticking paper back there," he says.

"What?" I yell in complete disgust. "That's so gross! No, I won't do that. Why don't you have toilet paper?"

"Jesus! Can you stop complaining for one minute? If you really need toilet paper, just go outside in the yard and pick some grass. But, be quiet. The neighbors complain over the slightest thing."

"You want me to pick grass?" I shockingly ask. My eyes feel like they're bulging five inches from my face. I feel delirious and desperately have to go to the bathroom. "Okay, you know what? Whatever. That's fine. I'll just pick grass. I don't have time to knock down a tree and make toilet paper. Be back in a few. Going outside to pick my T-P."

"Quietly, please!" King yells after me.

I exit out the front door and turn right into the well-manicured yard. I want to scream at the sky. I want to ask King a boat full of questions, but I feel my trachea and lungs constricting and slowing down my oxygen flow. That's always a sign that I'm getting too upset and need to calm down. Stupid asthma. I squat down toward the grass and hang my head between my legs. This position always helps me breathe better. I take a few big breaths while staring at a blade of grass. It looks so tall and sturdy and its color is a vital, tropical green. I think about a lawn mower cutting it down which makes me feel sorry for it. "What a brave thing," I say out loud. "You get cut, whacked, stomped on, shitted on, and sometimes picked for toilet paper, yet you always grow back. You're either brave or insane."

I'm talking to a blade of grass. I'm losing it. I chuckle to myself, pick the green blade of grass and a bunch of others. I head back inside the house to use the bathroom. King's busy fiddling with his laptop, so I quietly go into the bathroom and lock the door. While on the toilet, my phone starts vibrating. It's Haley. I stare at my phone but don't answer it. I don't want to talk to her or anyone for that matter. Both my dad and sister tried calling me earlier in the week and I didn't want to answer my phone then either. They both think I'm in Florida, or I guess, by this time, back in Philadelphia. I feel guilty about lying, but at the same time, I'm feeling better than I have in a long time. I feel like I'm living again and if I tell them the truth, they'll get worried and start yelling or lecturing over the phone. For the time being, I want to be cut off. From everyone but King.

26

"Becka. Honey, wake up. We have to be out of the house by 6am sharp," King quietly and sternly says while gently shaking my shoulder.

"Six in the morning," I groggily respond while yawning and rolling over on the air mattress. "Why so early? You might as well play reveille. Being with you is like a second boot camp."

"Honey, I have an agreement with the real estate agent. She wanted to start showing the house earlier to people, so we have to be out of it by six," King says while rubbing his legs with lotion. "And I need to roll up the air mattress and put it away. And when you're through using your travel bag, put that in the closet too. We can't have anything out and displayed in the open if I want to sell this place. But make sure you carry your valuables with you. Always have them on you. C'mon, lots to do, so get up!"

I groan, roll over a few times and gradually hoist myself up and out of bed. Well, it's not a bed. It's an air mattress.

King pulled it, along with a few blankets, out of an upstairs closet about five hours ago. I watch as King folds it up and shoves it in the closet. Then I feel something white hit me in my head and fall to the floor. It's a tube of lotion.

"Lubricate. Then we have to go," King orders. "Your skin looks better, by the way."

I grab the tube from the floor, squirt some lotion in my hand and begin rubbing it on my legs.

"My skin was never that bad," I comment.

"No, but you are prone to heat rashes and lubricating regularly will control that."

"It's because I work out a lot," I respond defensively. He's right, but it annoys me that he mentioned my heat rash. I look down and scan my limbs, fully expecting to see the red cluster of bumps somewhere, but I don't. I silently cheer. Maybe constant lubrication is the key.

"I'm guessing you don't shower here?" I ask, already knowing the answer.

"I only bathe in the ocean. Salt water is so much better for your skin. You should never use tap water unless you absolutely have to. But, since you don't go in the ocean…," King starts but doesn't finish.

"I do go in the ocean, but when it's warm. It's okay about the showering. I bought a monthly membership at the Y to swim, so I'll just shower there. Empty house, no toilet paper, no showering… why do you live this way again?" I ask. I start to wonder if I'm dreaming this whole thing.

King laughs. "Because it's a much healthier way to live than the way most of society lives. They are all dying. Look at me? Do you know many people who can keep up with me and do my workout?"

"No." And that's a very honest answer.

"So, you won't be joining me for my morning workout?" King asks.

"Not the first part. You eat and pray first, and that always takes forever. I'll join you after I swim. Swimming really helps my breathing, so I want to keep up with it," I answer while putting on a white t-shirt, black running shorts, pink ankle socks, and sneakers. King's wearing, as usual, his blue swim trunks and a big grey t-shirt that I haven't seen before.

"Alright, whatever you want. Let's go, honey. I want to show you my routine," King yells while trotting down the stairs.

"Your routine?" I ask while jogging down the stairs to the vast empty space below.

"Yes, baby. I'm going to show you how to live off the land. I'll teach you to be a true warrior. Just you wait!"

I smile when he says that. My body twitches with excitement as my mind perks up. His words sound like I'm about to go on a fun, mysterious adventure. It might turn out to be crazy, but I'm used to crazy by now. After packing my wallet, bathing suit, towel and water bottle in my backpack and hiding my travel bag in a closet, I follow

King out the front door.

It's 6:15am when we leave the house and still dark outside. The sun is barely rising in the distance and the streets are mostly empty. My sleepy feet scuff the sidewalk as we go. It feels like we're the only two people in the world who are awake.

As we walk down the sidewalk toward our workout spot, I start to see more people. Some are sluggishly walking their dogs. Others are dressed in business suits, sipping from coffee thermoses, and clumsily rushing to their parked cars. I watch an attractive girl fumble with her car keys then accidentally pour coffee on her white blouse. She curses and kicks her car tire with a black high heel.

"Wow," I mumble while still walking and watching the girl. "Poor thing, she has such an early work day."

"Ugh," King mutters in disgust. "No, honey. She's crazy."

"What you mean?" I ask. "She has to go to work. We all do. There's no free lunch."

"She's taking years off her life. Her mind and body are going to hell. Most people are mentally and physically disabled, indoors and outdoors."

I glance back toward the girl, who's taking intermittent breaks from cursing to drink coffee. Next, she lights a cigarette while wiping away at her blouse.

"She looks okay to me. Maybe irritable bowel. Maybe a little stressed. But who isn't today?"

"Give her a few more years," King says with a chuckle. "She's dying fast on the inside."

We continue walking down the sidewalk. Our pace changes from slow to brisk. I feel like I'm moving with a purpose, even though I don't have one. As I put one foot in front of the other, it hits me that movement, in general, is an antidote to depression. With each step, I feel lighter and livelier.

King suddenly turns off the sidewalk and down a narrow alley way. He walks up to a large green dumpster, opens the lid, and looks inside. A scraggly black cat meows and scurries into the alley from behind the dumpster, making my heart thump against my chest. I put my hand over my heart to slow it down, while King rummages through the bin. He pulls out a t-shirt, a sweater, a pair of jogging pants and two thick bundles of paper that he drops on the ground. Next, he holds a sweatshirt up to his body while announcing "This will fit." Then he bends down, picks up one of the paper bundles off the ground and begins rapidly leafing through it.

I stand still, my hand still on my chest, and stare at him. "King," I nervously gush. "What are you doing? Why are you going through a dumpster?" I think I know the answer, but I don't want to acknowledge it.

King laughs while still leafing through the mysterious papers. "Honey, do you know how much people waste? People are greedy and throw perfectly good things out. I don't have to buy new clothes. I can get everything right here. People are wasteful creatures. They think they need more than they do, when in reality, they don't. Don't be scared. Trust me and take a peek inside."

"You're kidding, right? You want me to go through a dumpster?" I ask incredulously. "You are completely insane."

"Scaredy-cat! When the world ends, the people who have no fear are the ones who will survive."

"If the world ends, I'm assuming I'll end with it."

"Just look. Make it a game. See what you can get for free."

When he mentions "game," I perk up. Even when I'm my most depressed, I can still manage to muster up a bit of excitement for games. I decide to take King up on his challenge, even though it seems like his whole existence is one life-sized board game, and ominous for that reason. Maybe I'll find something that will give me feeling again. Even if it makes me feel gross or nauseous, I'll take it. I'm a junkie for emotions and know it.

"Okay, fine," I sarcastically mumble. "I might luck out and find a used tissue or something. I can hardly contain myself."

Despite my fears, I inch closer to the dumpster. I peer inside and look around for rats and monster-sized roaches. When I don't see any tails, antennas or claws, I stand on my tiptoes, hesitantly stick my hands inside and sift through the trash.

The dumpster is full of a variety of things: food boxes,

wrappers, letters, broken toys, clothing and other bizarre house items. I keep digging through it, pulling random things out and dropping them on the ground. I find myself picking up speed. Soon, I'm completely immersed and preoccupied with digging through the trash. I'm overwhelmed with the desire to find a tossed-away, overlooked gem. My head is buzzing with excitement as my arms and eyes eagerly dissect the dumpster's contents like I'm on a wild treasure hunt. King begins looking through an adjacent dumpster, stops and holds up a pink t-shirt.

"Honey," King states, "look at this! It's a perfectly good shirt. See how people throw out perfectly good things? I think this one will probably fit you, too. Stand up straight, it'll make your belly look flatter."

I stare at the pink t-shirt and grimace as King holds it up to my body. I feel icky just thinking about wearing a shirt pulled out of a trash bin. I know I wanted to feel something, anything, before, but now feeling icky makes me want to go back to feeling nothing.

King sees my facial expression and commands, "Stop that, Becka! Have no fear! This is a perfectly good shirt. Have no fear, honey. God always provides! Don't waste money on clothes if you don't have to. That's what stupid people do."

"Yeah, but…" I start. "What about diseases and stuff? I'd rather wash it first. Is this where you get your clothes? You don't want to buy them instead?"

"No way. It's a waste of money. And the way I go through shirts, it's pointless. You need to get over your fears, or you'll never survive if something happens to you. This is a perfectly good shirt, honey. Plus, I know the difference between the gross dumpsters and the good ones."

"Are you seriously this crazy?" I ask with a nervous giggle. King simply laughs and ignores my question.

I freeze in place and study the shirt closer. There are no stains. Hell, the shirt could pass as brand new if I didn't know it came from a dumpster. I reach out, grab the shirt between two fingers and hold it away from me like it's a diseased rag. I inhale deeply, slowly remove my current t-shirt and stand in the alleyway only wearing my black sports bra and running shorts. I think about trying on the shirt. I really want to prove King wrong and be fearless, but the paranoid portions of my mind make me hesitate. I wonder if someone really gross or ill wore the shirt last. I wonder if the shirt is a vector for some strange disease that originates in dumpsters and makes your skin fall off. Eventually, I order myself to just do it. I tell myself that it's just a dumb t-shirt and can't hurt me. I take a deep breath and hold it, as if I'm about to submerge under water for a long time, and pull the resurrected t-shirt over my head.

Once I'm wearing the shirt, I puff the air I'm holding out of my mouth. My skin doesn't start to peel or itch, nor do I smell anything putrid. Gradually, I move my arms, shrug my shoulders and stretch the pink fabric to feel more comfortable. It actually fits perfectly. I smile victoriously, turn to King and ask, "Well?"

"Oh, yeah! There she is! There's my soldier!" King says with a high, shrill laugh. "It even fits! And you look cute. Compliments the blue in your eyes."

I giggle and jump with excitement in the air. Then I skip over to another trash bin and begin tearing through it. My brain's buzzing with a newfound energy so strong I can feel it tingling in the tips of my fingers and toes. Searching the dumpster feels like a game. It's like a poor man's treasure hunt, and I find I don't feel as depressed or emotionally dead. Dumpster diving as a quick endorphin boost and fast cure for depression? Shrinks would never think to prescribe it and shrinks, like many people, probably never dive in dumpsters.

"Come on, Becka!" King happily calls while interrupting my thoughts. "I'll show you another one. I knew you'd have fun doing this."

He's right. I'm having fun.

27

King, in his usual attire, and I, wearing my pink, secondhand find, continue walking down the sidewalk until he stops at another dumpster on the side of the road. I eagerly plunge inside and start scavenging through it like a hungry raccoon. King pulls out more bundles of crisp white paper and flips through them.

"What are those papers?" I ask while taking a break from rummaging through the garbage. There's gunk on my hands that I wipe off on my shorts. I'm officially homeless, I think.

"These are screenplays that people wrote," King replies while reading one. "The writers send them out to different agents, but the majority of them never get read. Most of them get tossed out in the trash."

"Really?" I remark. "That's really sad. A literary masterpiece might be in one of these dumpsters, and no one would ever know."

"It is," King says, almost begrudgingly, while tossing one of the trashed screenplays back in the dumpster. "The entertainment business is about who you know. But that's life, honey."

"But… you write, don't you?" I ask, remembering that he mentioned he wrote screenplays when we first met.

"Yep," he says. "But I threw most of mine out."

"Why?" I'm completely astonished that he would do such a thing.

"Like I said before, honey. Life."

I drop the subject as we begin walking down the street again. The sidewalks become more populated as the sun grows brighter in the sky. We're about to pass an expensive steak restaurant off the side of the road when King turns down a side street and briskly walks toward the back of the restaurant. He walks up to a large dumpster behind the steak house, opens its lid, and begins pulling out brown paper bags. He carefully places them on the ground. Then he slams the lid shut, opens one of the paper bags, looks inside and says, "Mmmm. Delicious."

I crouch down and open one of the paper bags. My eyes and nostrils are struck with the sight and smell of raw meat. The meat looks like a swarm of bloody worms. I quickly move away from the bag while suppressing my urge to vomit. "Oh my God," I comment while holding my hand up against my mouth. "Please don't tell me you eat that."

King reaches inside one of the bags and pulls out a handful of raw meat. He pulls out a bottle of hot sauce from the brown bag he's already carrying and begins dousing the raw meat with orange sauce. He shoves the hot sauce-covered raw meat in his mouth and starts chewing.

"I've been eating this for years, baby," King says while chewing the raw meat. "And I'm rarely sick. I never get sick. That's how strong I am, honey. And think of the money I'm saving? This is prime steak! The best of the best, and I'm getting it for free! Plus, raw meat is the best for you. People ruin this meat once they cook it."

Watching King devour the raw meat makes me want to hurl. Granted, he has one of the strongest bodies I have ever seen and obviously is eating the right foods to maintain such a body, but still, the thought of eating raw cow makes me want to faint.

"What about parasites?" I ask while forcing myself to look in the opposite direction of King. "The meat's not cooked. You can get worms and whatever else lives in raw meat." I have a temporary vision of a huge worm nestled comfortably inside King's small intestine. "Aside from eating dog crap, the easiest way to get parasitic worms is eating undercooked meat," I warn. "Then again, it is a sure way to lose weight."

"Yep." King chuckles and continues to wolf down the meat.

"So that's what you pick up in the brown bag every morning?"

I watch, curious about how it tastes. As if he read my

mind, he carelessly rips off a piece and drops it in my palm. I stare at the bloody raw mush in horror. Then I slowly lift it to my nose and sniff it. I quickly lower it. I lift it again, and this time I bite off a tiny piece. I chew, slowly and apprehensively, but can't taste anything. I fearfully wait for my taste buds to kick in. Suddenly my mouth fills with a bitter, raw taste, and combined with the cold, squishy feeling of the meat, I end up spitting it out on the ground. I keep spitting for a while.

"Ugh! Damn! Yuck!" I yell. "How the heck do you eat this?"

"Honey. You have so many fears," he says while chewing the discarded raw meat like it's a perfectly normal thing to do. "I'm fine! I'm the strongest man you'll ever meet! This is solid protein. Here. Try some more. It grows on you."

I back up farther away from King while violently shaking my head back and forth. "No. No. Absolutely not. I'll die. I'll stick to cooked meat."

King lets out a deeper laugh and says, "You wanted to die anyhow."

I shoot him an intense look. I never once made mention about wanting to die. Suddenly, a chilly wave ripples through my body. It's an ice-cold current that runs down my back and out my fingertips. "Why did you just say that?"

He doesn't speak any words to me. He winks and continues eating the raw meat. I'm hoping his remark about my desire to die is just coincidental, but something tells me it's not. Wanting to die is never anything I expressed to anyone. It's more of a wanting to disappear, anyhow. It's a dark feeling that travels with me, like an ugly, black mole attached to my body. It has the potential to be malignant and dangerous, but for now remains dormant.

I look at King again. I'm scared, yet his uncanny ability to know things about me without me telling him is fiercely attracting. It makes me want him more.

King wipes his mouth with his forearm and puts his hot sauce bottle in one of the brown bags he just pulled out of the dumpster. Then he takes the brown bag he was carrying with him on our walk and tosses it in a metal trash can. "That's so I don't pull out a bag I already used," he explains with a satisfied grin.

I weakly smile back and quietly say, "Well, another mystery solved. At least I know what you carry around in the big brown bag. Though, honestly, I kind of wish that one remained a mystery."

"Oh yeah?" he asks jokingly with a smile. "I get potatoes from them, too. Raw potatoes! They're healthier raw. Our food wasn't meant to be cooked, you know? Cooking destroys most of the nutrients." King pulls yet another clean-looking, brown bag from the dumpster. I look inside and see tons of potatoes.

"They look brand new! Why are they throwing them out?" I ask.

"People are wasteful, honey. I told you."

"Well, I'm Irish, so I have great respect for the potato. Here, give me one. I'll take one for the road. A raw potato isn't so bad."

"That a girl. Be brave."

"But King… do you really do all of this just to be healthier and save money? I mean, really?" I ask, hoping he says something honest.

"Yep. I do," he says shortly.

His answer doesn't feel right at all. Something is completely off about his lifestyle, yet, it's completely mesmerizing how he makes it all work. I have my doubts about who he says he is and about the reasons he gives for doing things, but I'm not going to interrogate him. I'm lying to him too. Maybe he is who he says he is, and I'm just conditioned to think his lifestyle is bizarre and weird. Besides, he's a lifeline. He's a game. He's keeping me from myself, which is exactly what I need right now. I don't need to know everything about him.

King tosses me a potato. I catch it with two hands, and put it in my backpack for later. He stretches his arms up to the sky and gestures me to follow him. Together we walk in silence toward our workout spot on the beach. Once there, he puts his bags in the usual corner. I sit down on an empty bench and watch as he prays for about five minutes. Next he runs over to the pull-up bar and easily does twelve pull-ups. Then he begins doing jumping jacks. I jump to my feet, wave, and begin walking toward the Y to swim. I keep glancing back at King. His stomach's ability to digest the raw meat so fast is amazing. He's amazing. He's not human, I think, as I walk alone to the swimming pool.

28

Saturday morning comes around fast. It's my second Saturday in California, which means that King and I have been together for a little over two weeks. We've spent so much time together though, that it feels like it's been much longer.

We are both resting on the saggy air mattress and staring at the high ceiling after making love. It's less awkward than before but still doesn't feel genuine. We connect, but there's an obvious short circuit.

"I'm the best! The best! No one can do it like me. There's only a few of us in the world, a few professional love-makers that is," he says while catching his breath. I roll my eyes, but he doesn't see. King never misses a chance to brag about his lovemaking skills.

"Then why not do that for a living? Instead of practicing law? Why not be a professional love-maker? What do they call those… porn stars?" I ask while continuing to eye the ceiling aimlessly.

"Don't be silly," King flatly responds. "I love what I do. I'm blessed for having such a great life."

"I'm not being silly," I shoot back and glare at him. "There's a lot of money in it. You know I read about this one joint in New York City where you can get five hundred dollars every time you let a man massage your feet. Yeah, men with fetishes will pay you to massage your feet. Don't you think that beats an office job? Hell, I'd do it, if it didn't seem so sleazy and my feet weren't flat."

"Don't talk like that, honey," King scolds while playfully swatting my stomach. "You're worth more than that. You're educated. Those women don't want to do that. They don't want to feel bought."

I stare in silence at the far-away ceiling while thinking about escorts. Of course, being bossed around sexually by men must ruin some girls. At the same time, they are getting money for doing what a lot of women do for free. What about the girl who takes drinks from a guy, gets duped into thinking the guy likes her, gets drunk and ends up having sex with a strange man who doesn't even call her the next day? I know a lot of those. At least escorts get paid for having sex, so in that sense, it makes them smarter than a lot of women.

"Hurry, honey," King says after pushing himself up and off the air mattress. He reaches for his shirt and pulls it over his head. "It's the Sabbath. I want to get to the beach and claim a spot."

I nod in response. Earlier in the week, King told me that he treats the Sabbath, or Saturday, as a day of rest. Absolutely no work is permitted. He told me that last Saturday was an exception since I was still new to California and needed to get adjusted. When I asked him what that meant in terms of our daily activities, he said we'd lie out on the beach all day and rest our bodies.

I glance outside the window. It's early, but the sun is already intense. It's going to be a scorcher, so I begin rubbing sunscreen all over my body.

Once we're dressed, we head out the front door and toward the beach. Along the way, I stop at a tiny shop to buy breakfast. King, as usual, doesn't want anything. He swears he's good with his bag of raw meat. After I buy a coffee and whole wheat bagel, I walk outside to meet King. I look around and don't see him. Stumped, I walk away from the shop and continue to look for him. Finally, I see him bent over behind a dumpster. Maybe he's sick.

"King! Are you okay?" I shout.

He ignores me but stands tall on his feet. When he steps out from behind the dumpster and turns to face me, I notice he has around ten newspapers in his arms. He smiles and walks toward me.

"What in the world?" I ask him.

"These are all the papers from last week. I'm behind on my reading and use the Sabbath to catch up," he says with a grin.

"Wow," I say while shaking my head back and forth. "And I'm guessing you didn't pay for any of those."

King doesn't answer. He chuckles, like a little kid who just played a trick on a parent, and starts walking toward the beach. He gestures me to follow. I shrug and run to catch up with him. Stolen newspapers and the Sabbath, a fun-filled day of irony.

Together we spread a blanket over the sand after claiming a spot on the beach. I plop down on a corner of the blanket and drink my coffee. My legs are throbbing and sore from King's workout regime, so I'm grateful for a day off.

King drops the newspapers on the blanket, shuffles a few feet away from me and kneels on the sandy ground. He starts chanting in a language I don't understand. His voice makes the syllables sound pretty and musical. I never pray with him, but I always observe him while he prays. His prayer ritual is entertaining. It's like a workout. He starts out by kneeling for a minute or two. Then he jumps to his feet with his hands straight up in the air. While standing, he yells words I don't understand and then he bends low to the ground and kisses it. He repeats the sequence four times in a row.

I'm amazed by what people do when they pray. There's always a ritual involved, much like there is in mating, as if the person saying the prayer is trying to entice God like they would a lover. My ritual is lame. I rarely pray, but when I do it's while I'm lying in bed at night. I hardly ever finish my prayers, because I'm plagued with a Catholic-school guilt complex. If I don't make mention of someone in my prayers, my brain will remind me and make me feel guilty. Then I'll mention the forgotten as afterthoughts. The problem is, I keep thinking of new things and people to pray for, like an uncle, a pet, someone else's pet, refugees who died at sea, a worm I didn't put back in the soil after a rain storm, and keep naming names until I drift into sleep. I rarely even get around to praying for myself. At least King's ritual is more focused and exciting.

When he's through praying, he sits down on the blanket, scoots over next to me and starts reading one of the newspapers. I roll over onto my stomach to try to shield my face from the sun and sleep.

It's too hot and sticky to sleep, so I decide to go for a short walk. King is still reading the paper. I mosey to the ocean's edge and let the water touch my toes. It's freezing, causing me to skip backwards. I whirl around and start to watch a beach volleyball game. The players are all blonde, tan, and spirited. They look as if they jumped right out of the sun and onto the sand. There are other spectators picnicking on a rainbow-colored blanket while cheering for the players. Everyone's so delightful. The scene makes me ache.

Since coming to California, I only talk to King. I feel like he keeps me hidden from the rest of the world, due to my own volition, but still I'm beginning to feel a slight craving for my old life, my life before him and before med school. I somehow lost that happy, hopeful girl. Right now, I'd give anything to play a game of soccer in the sand with my teammates from home. Maybe I'm just homesick. Maybe I'm getting my period. Maybe I'm getting better. Maybe I have reason to cry. I brush back a tear and make my way back over to King.

"King," I start while lowering myself down on our shared blanket. "Do you have any friends out here?"

Without looking at me, he says, "I'm beyond the age of friends, honey. I have acquaintances, but that's it. I'm all about business these days. I have to focus on developing my mind and my body. That's most important."

"Oh," I practically whisper. "So you never go out with friends?"

"I used to do that stuff. When I was younger. I'm not a child anymore. Most people, I can't stand."

"What about… dating? Do you date?" I ask, though I'm not sure I'm ready to hear an affirmative answer. I'm attached to him and know it will bother me if he says yes. Instead of answering me right away, he leisurely tosses his cell phone into my lap.

"Look through my contacts. See all the girls."

I scroll through the contacts in his phone and see about fifty girls' names.

"Wow," I say, a bit annoyed. "You certainly have a lot

of numbers."

"Yep. Until I met you, I had a big appetite. Now you're all I want baby," he assures me while lightly touching my arm with his fingertips.

"Why do you still have all these numbers then?" I feel unsure, maybe jealous.

"Baby," he starts, "I haven't called one of those girls since you've been out here. Not one. I can delete all of them if it makes you feel better."

"No, no," I answer with false confidence. "Don't. I was just wondering. That's all."

King laughs and takes back his phone. He sits down on the blanket, rolls over on his side and closes his eyes. I do the same, and before I know it, we both fall asleep in the scorching afternoon sun. I wake up an hour later. My skin is sticky with dried sweat, and I can feel the sun rays burning my scalp. I try to stay awake but feel lethargic and paralyzed by the heat, so I go back to sleep.

29

When I wake up the second time, it's early evening. My stomach is growling, and all I can think about is food. King is next to me, gnawing on a potato from his brown bag. It makes my stomach growl louder. He offers me half, but I refuse. I'm craving something greasy, so I run over to a pizza shop on the boardwalk, purchase a slice and devour it while strolling back to King. When I'm finished, I sit back down on the blanket and realize that I have zero desire to throw up the greasy combination of cheese, sauce, fat and oil. I don't feel anxious or a sense of urgency to sprint to the nearest bathroom and puke. I feel satiated and peaceful. It's the most normal I've felt after eating a meal in a long, long time. I can't even remember the last time I allowed myself to eat a slice of pizza. I feel so good that I skip in the air and do a lopsided cartwheel in the sand.

"What?" King asks while eying me curiously after I awkwardly land on my feet.

"Nothing," I answer. "Small victory is all."

King still doesn't know about my eating problem. I never told him, nor do I have the desire to tell him. I think he thinks I'm a picky eater, but that's the extent of it. While I stare at the calm, silver-sparkled ocean, it hits me that I haven't binged or purged once since being with King. It seems the urge to binge and purge fizzled away once I started following King and his daily routine. I don't know why. Considering how much time and effort I vainly spent trying to cure myself, having zero bulimic desires is a small miracle. I could be getting better, and that epiphany makes me want to joyfully explode through my skin. I feel like crying tears of relief and dancing a spastic jig, but instead I run out on the beach and do another crooked cartwheel. Then I sprint back to King and throw myself in his arms.

"What in the world, girl?" he says, obviously having no clue what just got into me.

"Big victory. I'm getting better. Kiss me!"

"Getting better? That's what I'm afraid of. Then you'll realize how crazy this all is."

I ignore his odd answer and he bends to kiss me. It's a sweet, light kiss. Then he suggests we walk back to his place before it starts to rain. I look up at the sky and see ominous thunder clouds gathering in the sky, like an army falling into formation. The breeze feels cooler as it picks up speed. The storm is only a matter of time.

We gather our things and head back toward the road.

Within seconds, the cool breeze transforms into a howling, spinning-wind monster. It's freezing, so I hug myself and trot on the sidewalk directly behind King. Suddenly the sky unleashes. Heavy rain drops slam on the pavement below like a barrage of artillery fire. Some get in my eyes, making it difficult to see. I squint through the storm and can't see another soul outside. A car whizzing by on the road splashes me with dirty puddle water and soaks me. I scream in disgust as I grab the edge of my shirt and squeeze it out to dry. I glance at the street and watch as beeping cars operated by impatient drivers speed by us. Despite the rainstorm, I notice that hardly anyone walks on the sidewalks in Los Angeles. In fact, hardly anyone walks in Los Angeles at all.

"King," I shout into the downpour and at the back of his head. "Do you have a car out here?"

"Yes," he yells back in an annoyed tone. "But I barely use it. It's in the shop right now. I'd rather walk!"

I laugh and say, "I get that. But I feel like no one walks in this city! We're like the only two pedestrians."

King briefly turns around to look at me and says, "That's because people are weak and lazy, honey. People are unhealthy. They should walk more!"

"Tha...tha...that's true," I stutter. Even my words are shivering from the cold.

By the time we reach his house, I'm drenched, a walking mop. Brown puddle stains on my legs and clothes make me look like a drowned sewer rat. King tells me to wait for him, while he makes sure the realtor isn't around. Once again, he slinks around the back of the house, while I wait out front. In less than two minutes, he opens the front door for me. I storm in, run upstairs and grab my bag from the closet. I strip naked, wet my towel in the sink and wash the mud off my legs. Then I throw another beach towel around me and dry off. Despite being out of the rain, I'm covered in chills and shaking uncontrollably, to the point where my teeth are chattering. King notices, puts his hands on either side of my towel and begins rubbing me up and down.

"Wow. You really can't stand the cold," he notes.

I'm feeling warmer already. "I know. I hate it," I stammer. His body against mine is like a furnace. "Maybe there's something off with my thyroid."

When I feel warm and dry, King pulls out the air mattress and lies down. I dig around in my bag for my birth control pills. I usually take them in the mornings, but this morning I forgot. I search for a good five minutes but can't find them. Panicking, I pour the contents of my bag onto the air mattress. Still, no pills. Then I begin ferociously digging through my backpack. Again, nothing.

"King!" I blurt with desperate urgency. "Have you seen my pills?"

"No. I haven't," he slurs sleepily. I'm so nervous that I shake his shoulder.

"No. Really. Wake up! I can't find my medication, and I need it! And my depression pills! Where are they? I can't even find my inhaler! I really, really need that. I'll have to fly home as soon as possible if I can't find them," I complain, starting to cry.

King forcefully sits up on the mattress, glares at me and spits, "Okay, okay, just shut up! I have them. They aren't good for you, honey. They mess up your menstrual cycle and make your body work harder than it has to. You don't need them. And the depression pills, they destroy your liver! And your lungs, if you let them, would get stronger on their own without your inhaler. Please, just trust me on this. And, though you're not ready to hear this, I want you to have my baby. That's why I took your pills. It's for your own good."

My jaw drops. I try to ignore my ears, but his words are like obnoxious, speeding trains through my auditory canals. My head starts to spin. I feel like I'm stuck on a merry-go-round that King keeps pushing around despite my hesitant wishes to get off. He's pushing it too fast and too soon. My hands start shaking. My breathing speeds up while the white walls feel like they're collapsing on me.

"No!" I scream and throw myself on the floor like a baby in the fits of a tantrum. Tears are pouring out of my eyes. "I need those pills! I need my inhaler! What if I have an asthma attack? I'll die. I need them! How dare you take my pills! And a baby? Are you fucking crazy? We just met, you don't even know me! I'm not ready to have a baby. Why would you even say that? Oh my God. Oh my God. This is crazy! What am I doing? I just want to go home."

King calmly runs his hand through his black fuzzy hair. Then he laughs, bends over and gently hoists me onto my feet. I'm wobbly and can't support myself. His hands remain locked underneath my elbows when he starts talking.

"Okay, please, just stop crying. Please. Baby, I shouldn't have taken your medicine. I'll give it back to you. Okay, Laura? Calm down. And look, you're crying now, but not having an asthma attack. It's because my routine is making your lungs stronger, baby. I'm only trying to help you! You're more fit now than when I first met you. You should be grateful. Do you know how much people offer to pay me for my workout plan? Tons! And most of the time, I don't give it away. Not that easily, honey."

"Why'd you mention having a baby? I can't do that," I whimper. Snot is dripping out of my nose.

"Relax. Please, just calm down. You're making me upset, too. We don't have to talk about babies right now. I guess I'm just trying to tell you how much I care about you."

No words form at my mouth, so I simply nod. When he mentioned the word "baby," I felt my entire body lock down in opposition. It all felt wrong. The men I know would run the other way if I said I wanted a kid, and that's because they are sane.

He finally hands me my pills and inhaler, which I snatch from him. "Who is Laura? Why did you call me Laura?" As soon as the question's out, my body braces for something it doesn't want to hear.

"No one," he quickly whispers and looks away. "You look like someone I used to know named Laura."

I slowly nod and don't bother to press the issue further. I'm already upset and don't need anything else to make me more upset. I'll remember the name Laura, though. That's for sure.

King walks into the bathroom and locks the door behind him. While he's in there, I put my pill bottles and inhaler in a plastic bag then bury it inside my backpack. After tossing a t-shirt and pants over my backpack, I drop down on the air mattress with one arm wrapped securely around my camouflaged bag. Sleep comes to me fast.

30

It's well before dawn, and King and I are sitting up on opposite ends of the air mattress. We're both silent and motionless as if we're waiting for our brains to wake up and operate our bodies. Then he stretches, yawns and announces that we have to can our morning workout session and walk to the Coast Guard office in Marina del Rey. He says he has to pick up paperwork concerning his father's estate, and that it's a long enough walk to suffice as a workout. I shrug, yawn and start getting dressed. His plans are my plans. Five minutes later, we're outside on the sidewalk, side by side, en route to the Coast Guard office. It feels too early for talking, so we both walk in silence. It's near light, and the pensive stillness that makes up the transition from night to morning causes my mind to wander.

I think about my lifestyle with King. We maintain the same rigorous routine every day, minus the Sabbath. I've only been with him a little over two weeks, but it feels like much longer, no doubt due to his intense workouts. Even though his routine is physically draining, it invigorates me. I enjoy waking up early every morning and looking through dumpsters on our walks to the beach. It's like starting every morning with the buzz of a scavenger hunt.

King's workouts are getting me in the best shape of my life. My body is harder and more toned. I've lost weight, am using my inhaler less, am getting more and more comfortable on the swinging rings, and I'm able to do two full pull-ups by myself. Simply looking better makes me feel better. My skin even looks better. King found a half-full bottle of lotion chucked in the trash bin, and we both apply it to our skin twice a day. He always comments on how wasteful people are with lotions, and he's right. It's remarkably easy to find half or three quarter filled bottles of lotion in the trash.

I'm also eating better and spending little to no money on food. I eat a lot of raw potatoes that I pull out of the steak restaurant's dumpster. They taste good—or maybe they just taste edible with a little bit of hot sauce poured on top. More importantly, they're filling and they satiate my hunger pangs. But my greatest achievement has to be that I haven't binged or purged once since hanging around King. I don't even have the urge. It feels like I traded in my mind and body for new ones.

King even convinced me to search for clothes, and occasionally I'll find a running shirt, a pair of shorts or a sweatshirt to wear. I leave the torn or stained clothes but relish the decent ones, which I wear to the beach, wondering why people trashed them in the first place. King still wears the same shorts every day and rarely switches out his t-shirts.

King's good for me. That's how I feel, at least. Sometimes I wonder if it's not him making me happier but my antidepressants. They should finally be kicking in about now. Either way, I'm sticking with King.

Part of me wonders if King's even real. I never met anyone like him in my life. I don't know another man who doesn't spend money, lives entirely off the land, looks like he could be featured in a muscle magazine, and is blissfully happy. Not one. That's why, at times, I wonder if I'm going crazy and if King is a hallucination my mind created. What if, after all this time, I'm the schizophrenic one, and not Chase? The thought makes me shiver.

Suddenly King skids to a stop, hits his head as if he just had an epiphany and says, "Oh! I have a surprise for you. You'll love it. Trust me!"

"Well, what is it?" I perkily ask.

"I have to take you there. What's today? The day, not the date."

"Wednesday."

"Perfect," he replies with a confident smile. "After I pick up what I need to get, I'll take you to a place you'll love."

Our journey begins by walking through the canals where

rich colorful homes and flowers line the narrow bodies of calm water. Then we hop on a sidewalk along a road with lots of traffic. Based on the way my legs feel, I'm guessing we walked around four miles. I don't mind, because the day is gorgeous: sunny and cloudless with a just-right temperature. King, who's a few feet ahead of me, stops again. He turns around to face me and announces, "I almost forgot! I have another surprise for you in my pocket."

"What?" I eagerly ask with wide, excited eyes. I love surprises. Well, the good ones.

King reaches inside the pocket of his blue swim trunks and hands me a rolled up piece of black lacy cloth. I unravel it and hold it up in the air to get a better look.

"What the…?" I confusingly ask while shifting my eyes back and forth between the crumbled rag and King. "A dust rag? A hair tie?"

"No, look closer. It's underwear!" King exclaims triumphantly, like it's the best gift anyone could ever receive.

I analyze the cloth closer while I'm holding it in the air. My brain futilely tries to make it into a pair of underwear. I flip it around and turn my head sideways to determine the front from the back. I'm staring hard but can't see it. There's something missing. When I realize what's missing, my eyes bulge out in horror.

"King!" I yell loudly and incredulously. "There's no crotch part! The crotch part is missing! What the heck is this?"

"That's the style," King calmly states while snatching the underwear from my hand. Neither his face nor his eyes show an ounce of emotion. "They are sexy. I wanted to get you something sexy."

"You wanted to get me something sexy, so you got me crotchless panties?" I repeat. My horror has morphed into disgust. "That's absolutely vile."

"You don't like them? Well, keep them anyhow. Maybe they'll grow on you. They're for you after all."

"Oh, really?" I ask sarcastically. "No, I'm fairly certain they're for you."

"No. They're for you," King answers evenly. He continues walking on the sidewalk and doesn't eye me once.

A bitter laugh escapes from my mouth before I say, "No, trust me. They're for you."

Having nothing else to say, we resort to walking in silence. After being let down by King's gift, I'm heated and walking faster. I'm also worried. He never spends a dollar, which means he probably didn't buy the underwear. That means he either stole them or dug them from a dumpster. I cringe. My stomach feels woozy. I'm okay with wearing old t-shirts, shorts and sweatshirts, but I draw the line at used underwear. That's just gross. Even though they aren't really underwear since they're crotchless, I'm still disgusted. I feel like taking a shower.

"King," I start calmly, not wanting to offend him. Maybe

he thinks his gift was great. "Where did you get that pair of underwear from?"

"Never mind, Becka. It was a present. You're not supposed to ask that question," he says without looking back at me. I may have detected an ounce of hurt in his voice.

"No, really. Did you get them from a dumpster? Cause that's just sick," I blurt out. I can't let this one go.

"Then be an ungrateful bitch!" King snaps with an unexpected burst of anger. He whips around to face me as I freeze on the sidewalk, fearful to take a step closer to him.

"Whoa. Sorry," I stutter apologetically. "I'm just wondering. That's all. It's no big deal, really. Thank you, then. Never mind."

He stares at me coldly for a few more seconds. I look down at the ground and feel like an ingrate. Damn guilt complexes. After taking a few deep breaths, I hesitantly start walking again, as if to show him I'm ready to forget about the underwear and move on. He takes heed, turns around and walks forward as I let out a deep sigh of relief.

"We're here," he announces as he stops in front of a brown brick building on the bay. "Wait here. This will just take me a few minutes."

"You don't want me to come in?" I innocently ask. Again, he's being annoyingly mysterious.

"No. Wait here. Sit on this rock, so I can see you from the

window," he orders. Then he turns and walks in the building. I shrug and begrudgingly plop down on a large, gray rock positioned amongst a variety of pink and purple flowers and stare intently at the Coast Guard's office window. I feel like a leashed dog waiting for his master.

Finally, I see him and two, maybe three, other men in the window. He waves slowly and purposefully at me, as if he wants everyone in the office to see him doing it. Automatically, I smile and wave back, while catching a closer glimpse of another man in the window next to King. He studies me with a strange look on his face. His expression is a mix of confusion, concern and anger. He's staring at me longer than a comfortable amount of time. Is he trying to tell me something? Do I remind him of someone? It looks like he's wearing a uniform of some sort, though I can't be sure from where I'm sitting. I feel uneasy and turn my head away. I stare across the street while my legs nervously jitter and a creepy feeling settles in my gut. Only a minute passes before King is back outside and standing in front of me.

"That was awfully quick," I point out while temporarily disregarding the man's odd look in the window.

"I just had to pick something up. That's all," he answers nonchalantly and walks by me. "C'mon, babe. I want to show you a cool place."

I hop to my feet and scurry to catch up with King. We start walking back the way we came, passing the same houses and stores we saw on the way here. I'm happy to be moving again, but I can't completely rid myself of the disturbing look in the man's eyes nor the creepy feeling slowly and steadily taking me hostage.

31

We walk another two miles when King stops, looks around puzzlingly, then exclaims, "Here we are. You're gonna love this, baby! The best bagels in the world!"

"Bagels?" I ask with the enthusiasm of a three year old in a toy store.

"You love bagels, right? This is the place to get free bagels," he explains while pointing to a small brick building with a hunter-green roof. "Follow me. I'll show you."

I eagerly trot behind King to the side of the bagel shop where a large brown dumpster is located. He lifts up its lid and pulls out two large, clear plastic bags full of bagels.

"Look at this, honey," King gushes while opening one of the bags. "Every Monday and Wednesday, they throw away the bagels no one buys. They're all in perfect condition! Here, have one. Take some for the road. There's whole wheat, banana, French toast, cinnamon, and more! And you get them all for free!"

"I love free!" I say with a delightful giggle. Every time

King teaches me how to score something for free, I feel like I'm winning, like I outsmarted an enemy, even though in this case it's just a store that bakes more bagels than it can sell.

I reach inside one of the plastic bags and grab a bagel. It's soft and smells fresh. I nibble at it cautiously. It tastes moist and doughy, which is exactly how I like my bagels. I bounce up and down with excitement. Bagels are one of my favorite foods and discovering that I can get a quality bunch for free makes me want to break out in a victory dance.

"I can't believe this. I can't believe they just throw these out!" I comment, while chewing a cinnamon bagel. "Can we come here every Monday and Wednesday afternoon? These are so, so good."

"Well, it's a bit of a walk," King remarks while sitting down at a small white patio table in front of the bagel shop. He's pensively studying me.

"I'll walk for bagels! I will," I yell before sitting down at the table across from King. After squirming to get comfortable in my chair, I continue eating my bagel.

He drinks from a water bottle, wipes sweat away from his face, clears his throat and says, "You're a lot happier than when I first met you. You look better and feel better. I'm great for you. You're not going to find anyone better than me. I love you, Becka."

I stop chewing my bagel when he tells me he loves me. My jaws feel paralyzed and my teeth, glued to the bagel bits between them. It has been a long time since I heard those words from a guy, and I don't know how to react. Two weeks feels too fast and too soon. At the same time, I don't want to hurt him. Plus, I need him in my life. I'm getting better because of him.

My heart quickens and my stomach burns from acid. I want to say the words back to him, but they feel counterfeit. If I really love him, those words should just slide off my tongue like rocks on a waterslide. Instead my mouth feels stuck, like it felt when I tried to tell Matthew I loved him. I stare at King's face but can't tell what he's thinking. He looks like he's contemplating his next move in a chess game.

"King..." I finally choke out, "I can't...don't make me..."

"It's okay," he interrupts. "You don't have to say it back. I know you're not the type of girl to say those words easily. But I can tell what you're feeling. That's why you're still here with me."

Oh, God, if he only knew. There's a huge difference between needing someone and loving someone.

Seconds later, a large black man comes out of nowhere and interrupts the conversation between King and me, and I couldn't be more grateful. The man is dressed in a black t-shirt, a black cap, and white jogging pants, and he's screaming and punching the brown dumpster full of bagels. He appears to be in argument with it. Suddenly, he whips around and stares hard at King and me. Then he slowly starts creeping toward us while screaming useless words in the air.

"Did you ever notice all the mentally disturbed people in the world?" I whisper to King while staring at the enraged black man coming toward us. "Should we go?"

"Don't worry," King says calmly, as he crosses his arms and sits up taller in his chair. "I've seen him around. He's harmless."

Despite King's assurance, the approaching man frightens me. I sense he doesn't want to make friends. I try to ignore him and pull out a small notebook from my gym bag. I begin scribbling and notice the crazy black man circling around the backside of King like a wasp about to sting. He still seems agitated and continues to mumble bizarre phrases under his breath. King is dissecting his bagel and not paying an ounce of attention to the crazy man.

The man starts mumbling louder as if he wants to instigate a fight. Then he stalls behind King and spits on the back of his shirt. I'm stunned as I watch a thick wad of white spit slowly land on King's back. King doesn't notice and continues picking at his bagel. I look at King and then down at his bagel. He's busy removing all of the raisins. I don't say anything at first, because I'm afraid of the fight that might ensue, but once the man walks a few feet away from our table, I lean in toward King and whisper, "King. That man just spit on you."

"Excuse me?" King growls in a monotone voice. This

isn't going to end well, I think.

"Yeah. I saw him. He was behind you and spit on your shirt," I whisper again with more urgency in my voice.

King's eyes fill with a ferocity that makes me feel like someone's about to get killed. He abruptly stands up from his chair, removes his t-shirt and sees the large damp mark from the crazy man's drool. With his shirt in hand, he confidently and slowly strolls over to the crazy man, who is now pacing back and forth in the parking lot.

"Did you do this?" King asks with a strong, angry voice while holding the wet t-shirt out toward the crazy man. "Did you, punk? Did you do this?"

The crazy man's answer isn't comprehensible, but King starts arguing with him anyhow as he jumps and lands with his feet staggered on the ground. His knees are slightly bent, and he assumes a threatening, closed-fist pose. The man is much smaller than King but approaches him regardless. He shoves King, who doesn't even budge. It's like watching a man push the side of a building. King pushes him back and the man falls to the ground. King straddles the man, squats down and starts punching him hard in the face. I cringe as I see blood splatter on the sidewalk and hear the defenseless, crazy man moan in pain.

"King! Stop!" I scream. I stumble over to his side and grab his arm. He shakes me away like a ragdoll, and I stumble to the ground.

"Don't ever disrespect me! Don't you ever!" King screams at the man while he continues to punch him in the face. His arms and torso look like a tornado engulfing the man's body.

"King! Jesus, stop! Please, stop! He's not moving!" I yell as panic takes over my body. The man's face is covered with a puddle of blood. He's no longer moving or moaning. I can't tell if he's breathing. King glances at me then back down at the man. He takes a deep breath and wipes his bloody fists on his shorts. He calmly steps away from the man. The man groans, and I sigh with relief. At least he is alive.

"King, King! We need to call someone to help him. Or tell the cops. We can't just leave him here," I say with a mixture of panicked authority and fear. My God, if I piss him off, am I next?

King doesn't respond at first. He calmly grabs his shirt, reevaluates the spit mark, shakes it out and puts it on. The man starts moving his head back and forth and mumbling incoherently. I can't take it anymore. I take out my phone to call 911 when King knocks it out of my hand. "What the hell are you doing?"

"Calling the cops. He needs help, King. We can't just leave him here."

"Do you want to get arrested?" King asks while staring right through me.

"What? No, I ...,"

"Then you're not calling anyone. Besides, he's fine. He's acting out, but I didn't hit him that hard."

"He has blood coming out of his ears, nose and mouth. I...," I stop. King walks towards me, the fury from before still in his eyes.

"Are you done?" He says while staring down at me.

My knees feel like they disappeared. "Yeah," I whisper.

"Good. I said he's fine, and he's fine. Now let's go."

I trek alongside King without saying a word. We walk thirty minutes in complete and utter silence. The sun, the silence, the warm breeze, the cars zipping by on the road and chirping birds combine to camouflage the horror of what I just saw. A man, almost beaten to death, is less than two miles behind us, and King is acting like everything's fine. I'm acting like everything's fine, just like I acted like everything was fine with Chase. I won't dare say another word, because I'm afraid King will hit me too. Or maybe I'll get arrested, like King said, for being an accomplice or something. Of course, I can't stop thinking about the injured man. I'm heavy with guilt, absolutely bloated. I shouldn't have said anything to King about the spit, but I had no idea he would react that way. If the man dies, it's on me, and now I'll never know. Maybe I'll read about it in the paper, and then King will be a murderer and I'll be an accomplice. Shit! I growl at myself and tell myself to stop turning everything into a catastrophe and that the man was talking and moving when

King was done with him. He was nowhere near dead. I need to let it go, or I'm next. The sun is starting to lower in the sky and the day looks misty, like a dream. Nothing feels real. I decide I shouldn't think anymore and focus on putting one foot in front of the other.

We walk about half a mile more when a Jeep with monster tires and chrome rims pulls over on the side of the road ahead of us. A colorfully dressed, handsome black man hops out of the Jeep and shouts, "Heya, King!"

King smiles brightly, jogs over to the man and gives him a hug. I stand a few feet away from them and watch as they converse in a different language. The man keeps looking at me over King's shoulder as if he's asking questions about me. I don't like the way he's looking at me at all. He keeps eying me and talking to King in a way that makes me feel like I'm an object up for sale. I feel uneasy and back farther away from the men. I hear King laugh and say, "Not her, man, not her!" As the man is getting back in his Jeep, he yells something in a different language, and King laughs again.

"What did he just say?" I suspiciously ask.

"Oh, nothing. He asked about you. Then he said every king needs a queen!" King cheerfully replies.

"Oh," I hesitantly answer while nodding. My gut tells me the man said something else, but I won't push the issue. I watch as the man's Jeep pulls onto the road and fades into the distance.

32

By the time we reach King's second home in Venice Canal, the sun slips from the darkening sky, like a soul leaving its body. The surrounding houses begin lighting up, room by room, as people prepare for their nightly routines. I study King's house, which remains lightless. It's clearly under construction. With its wooden bones and pastel blue tarps for walls and bright, yellow cautionary tape around its perimeter, it looks like a crime scene. King pushes one of the blue tarps to the side, stoops inside the wooden construct, and gestures me to follow. I hesitate but scurry in the dark opening after him.

It's dark, but I make out construction equipment, tool boxes, tool belts and saw dust scattered on an unfinished wooden floor. I carefully step around the piles of saw dust and carpentry tools and follow King to the bottom of a scary-looking, skeleton staircase that looks like a catalyst for breaking necks.

"Be careful, honey," King sternly warns as he cautiously

steps on the first stair. "This is really unstable so hold on. I'm not supposed to be in this house while they are working on it, so I didn't get insurance. If you or I fall, we'll be in big trouble."

I look at the wobbly wooden staircase and mumble with trepidation, "We'll get in trouble? More like we'll be cripples. Why don't we just sleep downstairs? I'm afraid of getting hurt and with my luck, I'll fall."

King's halfway up the stairs by the time I finish talking. He sarcastically yells down, "And do what? Sleep on a pile of saw dust? You're the one with the bad lungs who doesn't want to be inhaling that shit. I have blankets up here and cleared out a back room. Just be careful. You're a soldier girl. C'mon, honey."

I exhale a deep, defeated breath. Next, I motivate myself with silent reminders of being an agile athlete who can make it up the stairs. Without thinking, I'm suddenly rushing up the stairs on my tiptoes as if the stairs are on fire. I keep my eyes closed, half expecting to break a step and plunge to the sliver-promising floor below me. At the top of the stairs, I sigh with relief. I made it without any slivers or broken bones. I temporarily ignore the fact that I'll eventually have to go down the steps. I'll worry about that tomorrow.

From somewhere in the dark upstairs, King whispers my name. I quietly follow the sound of his voice to a tiny, dusty room in, what feels like, the back of the unfinished house. The dust triggers my asthma, so I instinctively pull my inhaler out of my pocket and take two deep inhalations.

"Honey!" King sternly scolds. "Why are you using that thing? I thought you weren't taking any more medication. I mean, look at me! My lungs are perfect, and I sleep in dust all the time. You just need your lungs to get stronger, like mine, and they won't do that if you keep puffing on that thing. The drug companies have you fooled. You just need to breathe deeper is all."

"Maybe," I softly reply. My voice is ripe with annoyance. "And I said I'd cut back on using my inhaler, but I didn't say I'd never use it. And I can't breathe right now, so I need it!"

"You'll be fine!" King snaps without looking at me. He grabs a few blankets from the corner of the room and neatly places them on the middle of the floor. "We have to be out of here by 5am, because that's when the construction crew comes in. I have a contract with them that says I can't be on the premises. Okay? So sleep in the clothes you are going to wear tomorrow."

"I can't change anyhow because my bag is at your other house," I mutter with resentment. "And no air mattress? We might as well be rats."

King laughs. "If you weren't tough, I don't think I could date you. I think that's the reason we get along so well. You're used to toughing it. That's the kind of girl I like, baby. I like warriors!"

"Maybe," I grumble as I toss and turn to get comfortable on the hard, cold floor. "Or maybe I'm just insane."

"Sleeping on a hard surface like the floor is better for your back and overall posture, honey. Beds are for weak people. You'll get used to it and thank me later when you don't have back pain and can walk straighter. As it is, you're hunched over like an old lady."

"No, I'm not!" I sleepily protest while trying to picture my posture and simultaneously stretch my arms and legs as long as they'll go. Maybe that will make me straighter, I think as I drift into sleep.

Before morning makes a proper arrival, I wake up to King shaking my shoulder. I wipe thick, crusty bits away from the corners of my eyes, take a swig from my water bottle, and mumble a few obscenities under my breath. It's pitch black outside, and I'm still exhausted. My body is sore from the floor.

"Honey," King says in his deep, authoritative voice while rubbing lotion on his legs. I told you why we have to be out of my house by 5am."

I grimace at the thought of forcing myself to get up and quietly whisper, "I'm just really tired and want a pillow or something the next time I fall asleep. I'll be ready to go in five minutes. I need coffee though, for sure."

After slowly rising to my feet and putting on my shoes, King and I carefully sidestep down the skeleton stairway.

It feels easier this time around, but then again, maybe I'm too tired to be scared of the death steps. We wiggle through a rip in the blue tarp and start walking in silence down a quiet road lined by motionless homes. Everything is still minus the shuffling of our feet against the gravel surface. It's breezy and dark out, dark enough to make me think I'm sleep-walking. We lumber lazily to the beach and drop our bags on an empty bench. King begins brushing his teeth and tells me he's going to jump in the ocean. I offer a lethargic nod, close my eyes and fall into a light sleep. Twenty minutes later, King nudges me as he's drying off and says it's time to walk to our spot. I stand up and we start on a silent, long walk. I only make one stop, at a coffee shop, and instantly feel perkier after a few sips of the black liquid gold.

Later in the day, like always, King and I are working out on the beach. It feels like our normal, average day. Both our moods are cheerful and don't reflect any negative energy from the awfulness of yesterday. We flirt and joke around for most of the workout and don't discuss the fight. I'm still thinking about the guy's bloody face, and I can still hear his painful moans, but I just keep it to myself and convince myself that he's fine. He might be sore, but he'll recover. I casually glanced through today's newspaper in the coffee shop and didn't see a police report about a beaten man in a bagel shop parking lot or a beaten man who later died at a hospital. I'm sure he's fine. Sore, but fine. But there is one thing I need to do to wash away my guilt and clear my conscience. When it's time for King to make his daily splash in the ocean, I tell him I want to go in too. It's my way of symbolically cleansing myself of yesterday's fight. I'll wash it off and have a new start.

"What?" he abruptly asks. His eyes are wide with surprise. "You never go in! You have a bathing suit on?"

"I know. But today, I want to. Don't ask me why. It's personal. I'll be fine in my t-shirt and shorts," I answer and jog with him to the shoreline.

I hope we jump in soon, so I don't lose my nerve. King holds my hand as we stroll through the shallow, freezing water toward the incoming waves, which are starting to pick up force. I glance up at the darkening grey sky, turn to King and announce, "I think it's going to pour!" I feel a pang of fear in my stomach. The last thing I want to do is get caught in the ocean during a storm, but I need to wash away the blood that splattered in my hair, the dried, smelly sweat of yesterday and, most importantly, my guilt.

"Probably, and soon," he responds nonchalantly, while leading me farther and farther out. The icy water is now up above my hips. I'm shivering, now, but King doesn't notice. He just keeps pulling me out deeper and deeper.

"Okay! This is good!" I blurt in a panic when I reach a point in the ocean where the water reaches my neck. The choppy waves rock me back and forth, making me feel completely out of control. I start thinking I might drown, get eaten by a shark, or get swept out to sea by a monster wave. I scan the water for shark fins or deadly tides, but I can't see anything. Everything is gray and murky. I can't take it. Screw the guilt. I need to get out of the water now. To make matters worse, my gut wakes up and reminds me that it's dangerous to be in the water with King. I silently scold my gut to shut up, but it doesn't. Stupid gut, it's like it has a brain of its own. This is awful, I think, as a freezing, cold wave pounds into the side of my neck. And King and I being the only two in the water while a storm is brewing overhead does nothing to ease my nerves.

"Dive into one wave with me, honey. Just one!" he shouts over the roaring ocean while gripping my hand tight.

"Really? It's going to start pouring any second. We should get out!" I yell over the growling waves.

"Just one. This next one! Come on!" King shouts as a wave approaches us. Right as he tugs my arm forward, I take a deep breath, tuck my head and dive into the wave. I'm only under water for a few seconds, and when I resurface King's hand is still clamped down on mine. His grip is so tight, it's almost painful. I glance back to my saving grace, the shoreline. It looks farther away than before.

While I frantically wipe salt from my eyes and mentally calculate my distance from the sandy beach, I feel my heart speeding. My breathing morphs into useless shallow gasps for air as I feel my lungs aching for more oxygen.

"That wasn't so bad, was it?" King asks while effortlessly bobbing up and down with the rise and fall of the water. He looks so comfortable, which makes me panic more.

"It was okay. But I'm going to swim back to shore now!" I nervously yell as thick raindrops begin falling on my head. Between the salt in my eyes and the rain, I can barely see.

"Just one more! C'mon. Might as well while you're out here!" King coaxes.

"No! I'm going to swim back!" I shakily yell while trying to wiggle my hand from his grip. "Let go! I want to swim back!"

"Are you sure you want me to let go? I can swim back with you. You're pretty far out," King placidly says while looking directly in my panicked eyes. His eyes are too calm and confident for the storm about to explode above us.

"NO! Let go!!" I demand more forcefully. "I want to swim! NOW! Let go!"

"Geez," King hisses and releases my hand. "I was just trying to get you used to the water, honey."

I'm too scared to respond to King. Once I realize I'm free, I push off the ocean's floor to help propel myself away from him. The waves are getting stronger, and the raindrops are hitting my head with greater frequency. Without saying a word to him, I start frantically swimming to shore with arrhythmic freestyle strokes. I probably look like I'm drowning to anyone standing on the shore, but I don't care. I focus on fighting through the relentless waves and keeping my mouth shut so I don't swallow salt water. I don't even take time to think. I just keep going and going until I'm there, until I can feel the sand underneath my body and am forced to stand.

I stumble in the surf a few times, scratch my knee, and by the time I crawl out of the water and run to shore, the rain's coming down hard. I squint through the blinding drops and try to find King in the ocean, but I don't see him. Maybe he's already on the beach. I shrug. Overwhelmed with chills, I sprint back to where we dropped off our bags and dig a towel out of my backpack. I drape it around my head to shield myself from the water bullets. A few minutes later, I see King. He's jogging toward me and yells, "C'mon, honey! It's coming down hard. Let's get out of the storm!"

I nod and start running with King towards the street. I'm soaked to the bone and freezing. I can't even feel my toes as I run. King comes to a sudden stop in front of a large, brown wooden fence. He peaks over the top and motions me over to him. I have to stand on my toes to see over the fence. A neat white cottage with glass doors is on the other side. I can't see inside, because it's dark and no lights are on.

"Want to get out of the rain?" King asks energetically. His face lights up with a devilish grin.

"What?" I ask him. I'm completely confused. "Are you suggesting we…? But that's trespassing. Are you crazy?"

"No one's home! We don't have to go inside. We can wait on the patio until it stops pouring. It has a roof. That'll keep us dry," King persuades.

I peek back over the fence and see a small concrete patio area with a tiny roof overhead. I suppose that will work. And I am getting drenched. Before I can make up my mind, King pushes himself up and over the wooden fence.

"C'mon!" I hear King whisper loudly from the other side of the fence.

"Shit," I mutter under my breath. Is it at all possible to avoid trespassing to get out of this storm? I remove my backpack and toss it over the fence. Then I reach for the top of the fence, push down with my hands and throw over one leg and then the other. It's slippery so I fight to keep my balance as I safely land on my feet on the other side. King's back is turned to me as he peers through the glass doors. It makes me nervous. What if someone is home? Or what if there's a guard dog about to nail us?

"King!" I call. "Stop it. Let's just wait on the patio and leave as soon as it stops raining. Please?"

King turns around, looks at me and says, "It's pretty nice in there. You sure?" I can tell by his facial expression that he's serious.

"Yes!" I shout with authority. "Knock it off!"

He laughs as I sit down on the concrete patio floor. A few seconds later, he sits down next to me to wait out the storm.

"You're no fun today, Becka. No fun."

33

It's maybe five or six days later. When you have nowhere to be, time blends together into a meaningless backdrop and loses its ability to dictate you. On one hand, it's freeing. On the other, it's completely disorienting.

Nothing big has happened. It's all been routine, with this morning and afternoon just like the last four or five mornings and afternoons. King and I woke up with the sunrise, went about our daily workout routine, ate whatever food we foraged, studied in the library, worked out again and now, with the sun setting, it's time to head back to one of his houses. I'm never sure what house he plans on going to, but I'm hoping it's the one that's up for sale and not the one that's under construction. My body is sore, and at least there's an air mattress in the house that's for sale.

King and I walk about two more miles when he stops in front of me, crouches down on the sidewalk and shouts, "A bird! Oh man, a poor bird fell from his nest!"

Right as he bends down to scoop up the baby bird, I

hear a chorus of maniacal, desperate chirping coming from a house adjacent to the sidewalk. I look at the house and above the door, in the roof's rain gutter, is a messy bird's nest. It looks like the mama bird haphazardly and rapidly linked any old twig and near-twig together to suffice as a nest. Mania's in the air, I guess.

"The nest is above that door, King," I calmly say while pointing to a tiny blue house. "Don't touch it! The mom will disown it if you touch it."

"Well, it'll die out here on the sidewalk. It needs a momma to feed it, but what would you know since you don't have a maternal bone in your body and don't want babies," King says as he walks towards the intense chirping.

"I never said I didn't want babies. I said I didn't want them right now," I defensively respond.

The mama bird's chirping becomes more shrill and intense as King steps up on the front porch stairs, stands on his tiptoes and peers into the rain gutter. The mother bird sounds frantic, as if someone is invading her home and about to kidnap her precious young ones. I see grayish-brown wings flap anxiously in the air. The mother bird darts out of the nest and perches on a nearby branch. Then she dashes over to the baby bird on the sidewalk as it opens its mouth wide and she drops what looks like a worm inside. King and I both smile. Mission accomplished, I hope.

"See? She'll take care of it. And it looks like it has most

of its feathers, so it'll fly soon," I say, satisfied.

King seems mesmerized by the baby bird. I certainly don't know everything about him, but he can't be that bad of a human being if he cares about a bird that can do nothing for him in life.

I watch as the mother bird speedily hops back and forth on the tree branch, all the while singing what sounds like a battle cry. She wants us gone. We turn to walk away, when the front door with the nest swings open. A large busty woman wearing a powder blue apron looms in the doorway. She's carrying a phone in one hand and a spatula in another. She shuffles closer to the door screen and glares at King. There's murder in her eyes.

"What the hell are you doing? Get out of here! Get out! I'm calling the cops! Get the hell out of here, you bum!" the fat woman screams.

"Sorry. Calm down. I didn't mean any harm. A bird fell from a nest above your door, and I was just helping it. We are leaving," King explains as he quickly backs away from her.

"I'm calling the cops! I've seen you around, and I know what you do. You're nothing but trouble! Get the hell out of here!"

King and I hurry down the sidewalk, away from the house and bird. We turn down a side street and take a different route than originally planned, just in case the woman does call the cops. Neither of us feel like being questioned by the cops. Questions are never good. We might not get in trouble for the bird, but we might get in trouble for trespassing, stealing newspapers or the man we left bloody-faced.

When we arrive at the for-sale house my heart's racing, and I'm sweating profusely.

"She was a nut, man. A lunatic! She's someone's maid or something. Christ, good thing she didn't call the cops!" King says with an amused chuckle.

"Yeah," I agree as I take a swig from my water bottle. "But in her defense, I guess I would be scared too if there was a humongous, strange man standing at my door on his tiptoes. I would have never bought the bird story either!"

King grabs the water bottle from my hand and guzzles away. When he's done, he lets out a massive burp and tells me to wait out front while he goes around back as usual. I still have no idea why we can't just walk through the front door of the house, but I'm too tired to argue.

A few minutes later, King comes back around the front and cautiously states, "Honey, there's a problem. We have to go to the other house. My real estate agent locked this house, and I gave her my one and only key."

"What?" I ask surprised. "What are you talking about? You were able to open the door countless times before when we came here!"

"No, I didn't. You don't listen. She would always leave the door unlocked in case I wanted to stop by, but this time she locked it for some reason."

"Well, just call her then, King. You have her phone number, right? My bag is upstairs in the closet! It has my books, camera, contact lenses, clothes and everything else in it. I need to get it!" I yell and start to panic.

"Honey, I can't get the bag and no, I can't call the realtor. It's too late. She won't answer her phone this late. By now, she's done working for the day. Stop complaining. Your bag will be fine!" King snaps back through clenched teeth. I don't know why he's getting angry when it's my stuff locked in the damn house.

"My glasses are in there! They're expensive!" I explain while starting to cry. I quickly dig through my pocket, find my inhaler and take two proactive puffs. King begins pacing back and forth and keeps telling me to calm down and be quiet. It's too late, though. Both my mind and body crack.

I stand on the tiny sidewalk in front of his big white house while tears pour out of my eyes. I stomp my feet aggressively on the pavement and whine about losing everything in my bag. I don't even know what I'm saying, or what I really want to say, but the words continue to fly out of my mouth in an illogical mess. I'm so confused as to why he can't just call the damn realtor and have her open the door, and I wonder why she suddenly decided to lock the house or if she even exists. I stumble closer to King, stand in front of him and scream, "This is ridiculous, King! Everything I brought with me to

California is in that bag! What the hell am I supposed to do? I have my period. I smell like dead fish and sweat! I want to change my clothes! Can't you just be normal for once? I want my bag! Screw you and your eccentric lifestyle and fucking nomad existence! I want my bag!"

King glares at me. He looks as if he's about to snap and possibly snap me in the process. He whips his head away from me, closes his eyes and inhales deeply, as if he's thwarting a violent reaction. Instinctively, I back away from him.

"Just get out of my face, Becka. And don't get in my face again. I mean it. Do not confront me like that," King warns. His eyes remain shut, as if he's trying to control his behavior with his words. "Just go out to the beach. Get away from me. I'll get your stupid bag. Just get away from me. Now. Do it."

Just like my gut kept me shore-bound when King invited me to swim in the ocean, it also keeps me from saying another word. I feel, smell, and see danger. Adrenaline suddenly controls me and sends a surge of energy through my body. My whine fest abruptly stops as my body's flight response kicks in. I'll cry and think later, but now it's all about getting away from King as fast as possible. I turn around and madly sprint toward the beach while King runs around the back of the house.

Once I'm safely away from King and on the beach, I bend over, press my hands firmly on my thighs for support, and take a few deep breaths. I'm shaking but feel calmer.

I lift my head and look around the beach. It's dark, chilly and windy, as if the weather is mimicking my mood. The weather's good at that.

I grab my cell phone from my backpack and contemplate calling my parents, Haley, or anyone from my old life. I'm guessing they are either worried about me or just assume I'm busy with school. Everyone probably thinks I'm fine and just being my usual reclusive self. Plus, my mom's so dramatic, I'll start a storm that will never finish if I call home.

Still, the longer I stare at the ocean, the more I ache to get out of here. I'm tired, confused and drained. My Philadelphia apartment has a bed, a tub, and even toilet paper. And I really miss my cat. I know my parents are taking excellent care of her and probably assume I'm too busy with school to drive to their house and get her, but those thoughts don't comfort me. The notion that my cat might think I abandoned her is pure hell. I desperately need to see her and hold her.

"Ouch!" I cry as something heavy and bulky rams into my lower back, causing me to thrust forward.

"There's your damn bag," King flatly says from behind me.

"How did you get my bag so fast? I thought the house was locked," I say, bewildered.

King steps in front of me, raises his hands above his head and smacks them against his sides. "You got your damn bag, right? Isn't that good enough? What else do you need? I got you your bag, so let's go sleep. I'm tired. You make me work for you all day long, and I'm tired. I've had a hell of a day."

"Okay. Okay," I answer softly. "I'm tired too. I was just wondering how you got it."

King bends over and touches his toes without saying anything. I stare at his body, which truly is a beautiful pillar of strength. It's one of those bodies that makes me both comfortable and uncomfortable. Very comfortable if it's my bodyguard but terrified if I'm forced to fight against it.

After King finishes stretching, he heads back toward the street. As usual, I follow. Only this time, while we are passing his white house on the way to his dusty wooden construct, I could swear I see two shadows inside the front window. What the heck? My gut tells me not to mention it to King. Instead, I glance at the phone number on the "For Sale" sign and plug it into my phone.

34

Once King and I reach his other house, he grabs a blue blanket in the corner of a downstairs room, throws it on the floor, lies down and falls asleep. I curl up in the fetal position, face away from King and pretend to sleep. I'm beyond grateful that he's so tired and doesn't ask to make love. I feel too whacked for any sort of lovemaking. For the first time in many nights, I'm thankful that we have to get up early and vacate the skeleton house, because it will give King less time to bother me about making love.

After a restless night of fragmented dreams, I hoist myself off the ground, change clothes in the far corner of the room, shake King's shoulder and whisper, "Hey. King. We have to wake up and go! Your construction crew will be here any minute. We have to leave!"

King breathes heavily, snorts and sits up on the blue blanket while yawning and pawing at his eyes with his large, black hands. "We don't have to go yet, baby. I want to make love. That's what I want to do," he grumbles sleepily.

"No, we can't!" I say urgently with a newly found, authoritative tone. "We have to leave. Seriously, your construction crew will be here any minute! Let's go. C'mon. You'll get in trouble if they see you here."

King doesn't protest. Instead, he groans and lazily starts getting dressed. I sigh with relief and feel satisfied that I dodged another potential moment of fake intimacy.

A few minutes later, we're dragging our feet through a dark fog toward the boardwalk. We both throw our bags on the ground and stretch our arms up to the sky. King uses an outdoor shower to wash his face and brush his teeth. Once he's done, he kneels on a sand-covered slab of concrete and begins praying. Everything feels routine, minus a knowing, sick feeling in my gut that I normally only associate with matters of heartbreak. Something bad's coming. I feel it, want to avoid it but know I can't. I'm also unusually slow and desperately want to take a shower. Maybe the cold water will wake up my muscles.

I glance around the quiet, dark boardwalk to see if anyone's around. It's empty and still, so I figure it'll be safe to take a two minute outdoor shower. I take off my t-shirt and shorts while forgetting that I have my bathing suit on underneath. It's still chilly out so I decide to leave it on. If it was warmer and the boardwalk stayed desolate, I probably would have stripped down to nothing.

Once I'm through with my shower, King is eager and

ready to start our routine. I tell him that I'm going to take a different route and walk to the Santa Monica YMCA so I can swim laps.

"What? You don't want to walk with me today? You're being lazy," King says. He's only slightly sarcastic.

"No, not at all," I assure him. "I just really want to swim laps today, and I want to get to the pool early so I get my own lane. I hate sharing lanes."

"Okay. Suit yourself. You don't want to go searching with me?"

"Um, not right now. If you find something really good that you think I might like, just grab it for me."

"Hey, hey! One man's trash is another man's treasure!" King chimes.

I wave bye, briskly walk away from King and turn down a different street. I feel energized and refreshed with a new sense of self and something that feels close to sanity but isn't quite it. Perhaps it's just motivation to get sane. I feel like my mind has entered a mode of survival and damage control, which I figure comes right before sanity. Then my mind would suffer from countless regrets, which would inevitably result in more damage control, and then who knows? I cringe and tell myself that I'll either cross or jump off that bridge when I come to it.

On the side of the road, I see a small coffee shop and stop in. I order a large black coffee, which along with my inhaler, seems to ward off impending asthma attacks. I take my coffee, sit down at a table near the window and watch as a gaggle of giggling girls happily saunter into a trendy-looking clothing store. My skin bubbles with envy. I wish I could join them and find pleasure in shopping and talking about guys, but I can't. I hate clothes and shopping. I wonder how it's possible I enjoy dumpster diving so much, but hate shopping for fresh-smelling, new clothes with normal people. Odd DNA, I think.

After taking a few more sips of coffee, I pull out my cell phone and scroll down in my contact list to the realtor's phone number. I stare at it, while grasping my inhaler in my pocket. Then I dial.

"Hello?" answers a pleasant, female voice after a few rings.

"Hi, I was just calling about the house at 201 Pacific Avenue. It's the big white house. At least I think I have the address right. Is it still available for sale?" I ask.

"Oh, yes! It is still available for sale. It's been on the market for some time. It's a gorgeous house. Great location, too. Very close to the beach. Would you like to schedule a viewing with one of our agents?" the voice inquires.

"Um, maybe," I hesitantly start. "Actually, though, I was wondering who owned the house? Are you allowed to tell me that?"

I hear the woman shuffling through some papers when she answers, "Um, just one second. I have it right here. Okay.

Here it is. It's owned by a Mr. Zack Russo."

As soon as I hear the unrecognizable name, I feel light-headed and a flutter in my heart that makes me gasp out loud for air. A sharp pain spreads through my stomach, as if a cannonball of acid just hit it. My palms break out in a cool sweat. The blow of the realtor's wake-up call makes me want to puke.

"Thank you," I manage to squeak while I hear my bronchiole tree tease me with an ominous wheeze. "I will call you back to schedule an appointment. Thanks again."

I hang up the phone and stare blankly out the window. My brain stops working, and I feel like my body's locked in a million muscle spasms. I take a puff from my inhaler and follow it with a slow expiration. Next, I scold myself by slapping my thighs and order myself to not get upset and cry.

Other customers in the coffee shop gawk at me with morbidly curious eyes. I figure they should. I'm sure I look like a freak, but I don't care.

I manage to down the rest of my cold coffee before I leave the shop and walk to the local library, only a few blocks away. There are two computers in the library, both in use, so I wait. A younger man in a suit is typing on the keyboard as a map pops up on the screen. I try to remain calm, but I keep thinking of King's lies. How many more are there? What am I about to find out? Jesus, deception stings. Why are his lies hurting me so badly? I didn't think they would, and right now I'd give anything or take anything to go back to not feeling a damn thing. It was all that sex and spending time together. I got attached to him despite myself. Damn me. I try not to cry, but the tears drip out of my eyes anyhow. I need to get on a computer fast.

35

"Excuse me," I murmur through tears while tapping the young man on his shoulder. "I'm so sorry, but I really need to look up the man I'm with." His eyes look confused and defensive before softening. He apologetically says, "Oh, sure. Go right ahead. I just had to print out directions for a job interview."

He abruptly hops out of the chair, pulls it out for me, and offers a sympathetic smile. I slide into the computer chair, wipe the tears away from my eyes and type King's full name into the search box. A bunch of blue blurry links pop up on the screen, so I wipe my eyes a second time to see them clearly. At first, I feel a wave of relief, because most of the links deal with court cases, which makes sense since King's a lawyer. Then I look closer and notice one link that puts his name first, followed by "versus the city of Santa Monica." I take a deep breath, click on the link and begin reading. After two paragraphs, I feel increasingly dizzy and worry I might vomit all over the computer screen. This isn't happening. Not to me.

As I read on, I feel my gut muscles tightening into knots, threatening to hold me hostage in the library chair. My nerves feel like sponges as I become saturated with fear and anxiety. I click on a few more of the blue links and look at the blurry words, even though I'm incapable of digesting everything I read. My brain is pointless now. One link still manages to make my blood curl. It makes me want to claw at my face and peel my skin off. I click on it and read the following:

"Plaintiff was arrested on twelve occasions and was convicted at least nine times of various crimes. On November 24, 2000, plaintiff was convicted of sexual battery, false imprisonment, and molesting a child. He unsuccessfully appealed."

I stare motionless at the screen as my mind transforms into a whirlpool of darkness. I feel removed from the words on the computer, like I'm bored and reading about a distant sex criminal to pass the time. And even though I feel the urge to turn off the computer and deny everything I just saw, I know reality's harsh seed has been planted in my mind. There's no escaping it, and it's only a matter of time till the horrific truth blossoms inside me. I only keep breathing because it's automatic.

Could it be that I'm with a rapist? This can't be real. The tears stop flowing for a second as I contemplate the fact that

King's a rapist. This is absurd. He might be a liar and a thief, but a rapist? I certainly never saw him rape anyone, and he never raped me. There are very little details about his crimes, but I click on a few more links and figure out that King goes to court, because he's appealing the judges' verdicts on each of his cases. He represents himself without an official attorney. That's probably why he calls himself a lawyer.

My heart's thumping hard, my eyes are glued open, and I nervously keep glancing around the library as I read on. I'm fearful that King will sneak up behind me. Rationally, I know he's still at the workout spot, but my paranoia isn't convinced. Lord knows what he'll do to me once he learns that I know the truth. I do a brief search for alumni from NYU law school and, as expected, I don't find King's name listed. I look up home addresses for him and find a recent one listing an apartment in West Hollywood. The other occupant listed is a woman named Laura Johnson. Laura. Shit. That's the name he called me.

I do another online search for Laura Johnson and find a current address listed in Portland, Oregon, along with a phone number. I plug the number into my cell phone. Then I search King's name again and another link catches my eye. It's for the California Sex Offenders Registry. I click on the link and type King's name in the search box. His picture pops up on the screen, his location listed as "Transient." His age, height and weight are accurate. His crimes are listed as sexual battery involving a restrained person and molestation of a child.

I sign off the computer and hurry into the rest room. I unsteadily walk into the last stall, lock the door behind me, kneel in front of the toilet bowl like I worship it and make myself vomit whatever contents are in my stomach. At first, the sensation feels foreign, but then my mind quickly recognizes it and begs for more.

36

After vomiting, I silently praise God for the resultant calming effect. My throat starts burning, probably because I didn't have much in my stomach except coffee and acid. My poor, poor esophageal lining. I take a few deep breaths and leave the stall to grab a drink from the library water fountain. Water should help neutralize the acid eating my throat, but honestly, I don't mind the burning feeling. I'll take it over the anxiety.

Once I'm through drinking, I wonder what I should do next. Shock and puking seem to have suppressed my emotions enough to jar my body into flight mode. I have no time to think. I can only focus on damage control, and to do that, I must remain calm.

I leave the library and, while pacing up and down the sunny Santa Monica sidewalk, decide to call the phone number I found for Laura.

"Hello?" a female's crackly voice answers.

"Hi. I'm really so, so sorry to bother you," I nervously

stutter. "Um, but I'm looking for a girl named Laura. Is that you?"

"Oh, no. I'm Laura's mother, Ruth. She doesn't live here. Who's this?" she asks.

"My name is Becka. I'm actually in a lot of trouble. I'm calling from Los Angeles. Do you know someone named King?"

The phone goes quiet for a while. I think she hung up on me.

"What? How did you get this number? I haven't heard that name in ages. He's a horrible human being and very dangerous. That man hurt my daughter so badly, I can't even tell you. She wasn't herself when she was with him," Ruth emphatically exclaims.

"They lived together? Were they married? How long ago were they together? I'm so sorry for asking all of these questions. But I've been hanging out with him and just saw his criminal record," I admit shakily.

"What? Oh my God! He's a horrible man. No, he wasn't married to my daughter, but they lived together until the night he went to jail. I never liked him. Laura was way too good for him, but she acted like she was possessed by him. He's the devil. He would stay in that apartment all day long and do drugs while she worked. He wouldn't even watch the kids for her. She would have to bring them to work and put them in a playpen. You need to get away from him fast," she exclaims. Her voice is laced with venom.

"He went to jail the night he hit Laura?"

"Oh, yeah. He was in jail. That scumbag came home one night and beat Laura so badly that she couldn't walk for almost a month. He broke her ribs. He also threw his own daughter against the wall. And she's beautiful. I love my granddaughter. Good god, she's so beautiful, I know he would try to have sex with her. He ran a prostitution ring, you know? He and his sick friends had air mattresses in foreclosed houses. We knew all about it, but Laura was blind. He went to jail for almost two years. I wish he was still in jail. You need to get away. Don't walk, run!"

When she said "air mattresses" and "prostitution ring" I felt dizzy. That's how he has money and why he has so many girls in his phone. My mind shot back to when I saw two mysterious shadows in the white house and to when the man hopped out of his jeep and asked King about me. I was spared, but I don't know why.

"He has kids? He had kids with Laura? How many?" I ask while sitting down on a street because my knees feel too unstable to stand.

"Beautiful kids! One girl and one boy. The daughter is just like my Laura, a beautiful brunette with the sweetest blue eyes. I can't believe that monster tried to hurt her. The boy has behavioral problems, though, no doubt from him. He has attention deficit and emotional issues. All of his teachers want to get rid of him."

"Oh my God," I whimper. "I had no idea. Is Laura okay now?"

"She's okay. She hasn't seen him since that night he beat her. My husband and I drove down there from Oregon, put her and the kids in the car and drove them home. She lives in a neighborhood right now that is full of FBI agents, so if that bastard ever tries anything, we'd get him. My husband would kill him. He has sex with men, too, you know. If I were you, I'd get tested. He's sick. It's a shame they ever let him out of prison."

"Get off that phone!" I hear an angry male voice shout at Ruth. "Who the hell are you talking to? I told you never to talk about him. Get off the phone!"

Before I can say or ask anything else, Ruth or someone else hangs up the phone. I sit down on the street curb, tightly clutch my gut and stare at the bottom edge of tires whizzing by me on the road. I can't move. When Ruth said that King had sex with both men and women and suggested I get tested for diseases, my body froze in place. He was in jail and possibly bisexual, so statistically I know he's a likely candidate for HIV. I picture my blood being saturated with a billion viral particles, causing it to slow down to the rate of viscous sludge. I really can't move. I don't even know if I'm breathing. And the girls. And the air mattress. And that man who hopped out of the jeep and violated me with his perverted eyes. I feel like I'm shutting down and turning into a gargoyle on the street curb. Maybe that's the epitome of rock bottom: You become hardened to death.

I don't know how long I've been sitting here. I can't tell if I'm in shock or surprisingly calm. My military training programmed me from day one to fight when under fire and to function under pressure. Sometimes I think I'm most alive and at my best when someone's threatening me, because that's how I'm programmed. Is it possible that the fear of being murdered or beaten by a madman, one whom I entertained because of my own madness, can guide me back to sanity? To a safe place? Is fear a friend after all? Is the fear of losing everything the way back to a functioning, normal life? Oh, God, please give me a second chance. How I've fallen! I know I was unhappy in Philadelphia, but this…this is much, much worse. This is throwing my life in the dumpster. This is gambling with the Devil. This is death. Even if I get away from King, I still may die if he gave me HIV. He picked me as his queen for his deluded Manic Kingdom because I was perfect for it: a lost, depressed, lonely soul, and he knew it. Perfect for molding, probably like a lot of the girls in his phone. Why he spared me from his disgusting sex market, I don't know. Is it possible that he loves me? He never hurt me. Ugh, wake up, Becka! Stop being stupid! There is no love in Manic Kingdom. It's all lies and only lies.

A car honks loudly and spooks me. To the cars whizzing by, I must look odd and ill, like a rabid raccoon out during the day. More cars and minutes pass. The sun is dropping in the sky, so I guess it must be close to evening. I push myself off the curb, stand tall and stretch. I start walking toward the workout spot, one foot in front of the other. Each time my foot touches against the pavement, my thoughts become clearer and less scary. The mode is survival. My mind and body are robots equipped with shock repellants, like a soldier's. With each step, I strategize how I will get away from King and out of Los Angeles. I need to get my bag, which is at the house under construction. I need to be smart. I need to play it cool. I need to beat him at his own game.

37

After walking a few more blocks, I feel surprisingly calm and unafraid. A refreshing breeze, carrying the enticing fragrance of baked goods, caresses my face as I continue to put one foot in front of the other. "Remain calm," I tell myself. "If you stay calm, nothing bad will happen. You have been with him for a long time and nothing bad happened to you. It will be okay."

Five minutes pass before I see King. He's only wearing his blue swim trunks and moseying up a hilly street, no doubt worn out from his workouts. I continue to walk toward him at a confident, steady pace, like a fighter programmed for a specific mission. When he sees me, he waves, and I reflexively smile and wave back. He stops walking and leans against the side of a brick building to wait for me. I take a deep breath and when I'm finally about a foot away from him, I stand still on the sidewalk, cross my arms, and whisper, "Hi."

King drinks from his water bottle, offers me some, but I refuse. I study his perfectly carved figure and each muscle bulging underneath his smooth brown skin. I feel slightly relieved, because I don't think a man burdened with sexually transmitted diseases, mainly HIV, could work out so much and look so good. King catches me staring at him. His posture stiffens and his mouth tightens.

"What?" he asks flatly while taking another sip from his water bottle. "What happened? You aren't yourself. You've been gone a long time. I called you and no answer."

He's already noticing that something is off. I have to do better.

"No, I'm good. Yes, went swimming and then walked around a few stores. Sorry, I turned my phone off in the locker room and left it off." I force a smile.

"You hungry?"

"No. Not really. I'm tired though."

"Okay. Let's walk and go to bed early. If that's what you want," he says.

"That's what I want."

We walk in silence towards the house under construction. The evening is warm and calm, nothing stormy or out of the ordinary, as if the weather is cooperating with my plan. We get to the house, carefully make our way up the skeleton staircase and into the back room. King drops his bags and grabs his lotion. I study him as he rubs lotion on his skin like he's polishing the world's finest gem. I think about his criminal record. On paper, he's a rapist. A monster. And yet, right now, I don't feel afraid. If anything, I feel heartbroken.

He bends over and begins lubricating his legs. I think about the first time I saw him doing bear crawls and how I started doing them every day now. They really are a tremendous strengthening exercise for your back. I think about his crazy routine that he needs to do to survive, and yet he makes it into a fun game. I think about how I haven't puked in a long time, the good shape I'm in and how my depression got better. His routine is the biggest part of my healing process, and for that I will be forever grateful. No one, not even my doctors nor therapists, made me stop puking or feel better. I think about the time he wanted to save the injured baby bird. Yes, he's a monster on paper. But he's not all monster in the flesh.

He rolls out the blanket and lies down. "Good night, baby," he murmurs sleepily.

"Night," I say with a shaky voice as my eyes well up with tears. Do not cry, Becka. Tears will give you away and ruin everything. Things need to be normal for you to escape.

King's snoring soon fills the room. It's louder than ever. I'm wide awake, dressed in a baggy jogging suit with my sneakers on. I'm crouched in the corner of the room, hugging my knees to keep warm. A few more minutes, I tell myself. King's lubricated, muscular chest smoothly rises and falls. It glistens like chocolate candy, even in the dark. I wonder what will happen when he gets older and his chest isn't so muscular, and he can't physically keep up with his routine. It's not like anyone will hire him. He won't be able to get as many girls. Society is not going to give him, a registered sex offender, a second chance. Part of me knows he has to do what he's doing. He needs to lie. He needs his delusions to live with himself and stay alive.

I'm losing my nerve. There is zero room for second guessing. Now is go time. I quietly stand up and put my travel bag around my shoulder. King doesn't budge. I suck in my abs, tiptoe out of the room and down the stairs. Once outside, I start jogging in the chilly night. Then I start running towards the main road where I'm praying I find a cab. A few cars fly by, when like a sign from God, a cab appears. I start waving my hands in the air to get the driver to pull over. I jump in and ask the driver to take me directly to the airport. Inside the cab, I leave out a huge sigh of relief along with a few tears. I silently praise myself for not botching up my escape plan. It was so simple, not much of a plan really. King is addicted to his routine and gets irate when anyone or anything interferes with it. I wasn't about to interfere with it by having a useless confrontation which could have cost me my face or my life. I forced myself to contain my emotions and impulses in a way that wouldn't alarm or disturb him and then, as he slept, slipped out of his life forever.

The tears come faster now, because I let them. It's safe

to cry here. My upper body tremors violently as I bite my knuckles and sob into my fist. I roll down the window and let the night breeze cool my face. I feel exhausted suddenly. I don't know how it will feel to be back in Philadelphia or how I will even begin to collect the pieces of my life, but I'm committed to putting those pieces back together and right now, that's all I need.

"You know something?" the cab driver says while looking at me through the rear view mirror, as signs for the airport wiz by. "Your eyes look beautiful when you cry."

I half giggle and half snort. I think my eyes look their best when I'm crying too.

38

The next morning, I'm back in my apartment in Philadelphia. I feel dazed, like I just walked off a rollercoaster ride. I realize I might feel this way for a while, but I also must function. I need to pay bills, pay my rent, contact my parents, get Moses back and schedule a meeting with the dean to beg him to let me finish school. But first, I need to get tested. I fell asleep on the return flight and had a nightmare about getting HIV. Laura's mom was in my dream, standing over me and begging me to get tested. I woke up sweaty and anxious and nowhere near brave enough to figure out what I will do if I test positive. I'm still anxious, almost to a toxic level, but I know that I must force myself through the motions and get tested, otherwise anxiety itself will kill me.

I change into a new pair of jogging pants and a sweatshirt while checking the messages on my phone. King called me ten times and left three messages. I sigh and force myself to block his number. Nothing good will come of talking to him. Not now, not ever, not even when I miss him. Besides, he'll find a new girl soon enough and be too busy conning her to call me. Reminding myself that I wasn't special, that I was just one of many girls he fooled, helps me block him. Forget him and his lies, I think. The sad part is I can tell myself how awful he is and that I'm lucky I escaped, and even then, it still stings. I sigh and call my Indian friend, Amir. At the moment, I have whales to fry.

Amir, a total depression case himself, is one of my med school classmates. Over the last two years, we've become good friends, the type of friends who share the most messed-up thoughts with each other without the fear of being judged. It's comforting to have him.

"Hello," says a flat voice with a slight Indian accent.

"Amir!" I practically scream into the phone. "I know this sounds weird, but I need to get an HIV test. I have a major problem. Problems, actually, but I need to get checked now." I feel sick saying those words and refuse to allow my mind to begin imagining a life with HIV. That image is something I can't handle.

"What? Why? Did you stick yourself with a needle? I wish I had AIDS. I hate my life. Let's have unprotected sex," Amir somberly remarks. I wish I could slap him.

"No, I'm serious. I didn't get stuck with a needle. I had sex with a homeless guy who has sex with men. And he was in jail. He's so high risk. Oh my God. Oh my God!" I cry in panic as if saying it out loud increases my chance of getting it.

"You what? Are you joking? Who does that? I don't know anyone like you. You are completely insane. A homeless man? Were you on drugs? Okay, okay. Calm down. The virus transmission rate is really low. Like, less than one percent per sexual encounter. Just stay calm. I'll pick you up within the hour. I know a clinic in West Philadelphia that does the rapid HIV test. You can get results within the hour."

An hour later, Amir picks me up in his rusted red Honda Accord. He's wearing a jet black jogging suit and has a coffee thermos tucked between his legs. I crumble into the passenger seat when he comments, "Wow. Your energy is whacked today."

I throw him a nervous glance and snap, "Well, wouldn't yours be if you were on your way to find out if you had AIDS?"

"Not really," he says while pulling out of my apartment complex's parking lot and turning on to the freeway. "Did you do it in a cardboard box? Do I have a chance with you now?" I can't tell if his last question is partially serious, but I want to punch him.

"No," I whine while pulling my hair into a pony tail. "He squatted. Listen, if I talk about this, I'll explode. Can we just listen to uplifting music and not your usual slit-my-wrist stuff?"

Amir switches the radio station to oldies music and turns up the volume. He drives to the clinic without saying another word to me. I keep my arms folded on my abdomen in an attempt to calm down. My intestines feel like they might burst out of my abdomen, like terrified snakes looking to escape. At least the music is cheerful.

After fighting for a parking spot on a busy Philadelphia street, Amir and I silently walk to the clinic, only a short block away. We go inside and robotically approach a woman behind a receptionist desk. She barely glances at us before handing us two numbers and ordering us to sit in the waiting room till our numbers are called. I feel like I'm ordering lunchmeat. I'm surprised Amir takes a number, since I figure he's only here as moral support.

"Why are you getting the test? Are you having risky sex?"

"No. I haven't been laid in four years," Amir flatly replies while looking at me with his token somber stare. "I dunno. Maybe I'll get lucky."

I shake my head back and forth before commenting, "You are totally addicted to morbid things."

"Yes. By the way, you heard about Chase?" Amir asks.

"Chase? No. What?"

"He got kicked out of school. He's in a maximum-security psych ward now."

My heart sinks a little. Oh, Chase. Poor Chase. I don't have the brain cells to process what I just heard. I'm too nervous about my current predicament. I have to stay focused on myself.

"I didn't know that."

"Yeah. It's probably for the best."

"Number 35!" a woman dressed in all white yells as she holds open a door leading to a long corridor.

"That's me!" I nervously say while simultaneously jumping out of my chair and knocking it over.

"Just go. I'll get that," Amir says.

The woman motions me to follow her down the hallway and into a small examination room. I sit down in an uncomfortable plastic chair and watch the woman put on rubber gloves. She methodically reaches for a needle and a test tube on a small white cart. When I see the needle, my heart rate picks up. I absolutely abhor needles. I squeeze my eyes shut as I feel her tie a band around my forearm and tap around for a vein. She sticks me, it doesn't hurt at all, but I wince anyway.

The woman now holding my fate in a test tube tells me to sit in the waiting room for about an hour while my results are processed. I thank her and shuffle back to the dingy waiting room. Amir is already sitting in one of the chairs and staring blankly at a happy old-time jazz band playing on a bulky, ancient TV. He has a fresh band aid on his inner forearm, so I guess his blood was already drawn. The TV is on a wobbly coffee table that looks like it's about to collapse. Like me, I think.

Since I'm forced to wait, I watch the jazz band members, dressed in identical black tuxedos, dance around on stage while playing upbeat, cheerful tunes on their instruments. Every now and then, they take a break to smile and wave at an invisible audience. They have no idea they are entertaining people who might receive a death sentence within the next hour.

About five other people, all men, are slumped down in variously colored, cheap plastic chairs throughout the waiting area. Some are dozing and some are lazily eying the TV. All of them are emaciated and wearing dirty clothes. Glancing at their arms, I notice some with obvious track marks from years of drug abuse. They all seem bizarrely calm and sleepy, as if a diagnosis of HIV doesn't make an ounce of difference in their lives. They look like patients in a mental asylum, and I cannot believe I'm sitting here with them. "Please, God, let this all be a nightmare," I pray. I don't belong here. I'm not one of them. It's a mistake. These people and this room don't feel real to me. They're fragile shells of humans lost to apathy a long time ago. More than ever, sitting here, I am begging for a second chance.

"I don't think I can take this anymore. This music is driving me nuts," I complain. My legs start shaking uncontrollably. I'm about to lose it. If anxiety can kill, I'll be dead within the next hour. With each minute that passes, I grow increasingly dizzy as the room feels more and more surreal. I keep staring at the clock hanging above the TV in the waiting room while biting my nails and begging the floor to open up and swallow me.

My heart and mind are speeding beyond my ability to slow them down. I try to calm down by taking long inhalations and exhalations, but they don't work. Screw yoga. Screw meditation. None of that stuff works when I really need it. I glance at the clock again. It's going so damn slowly that it might as well be going backwards. I sit on my hands to suppress the urge to rip it off the wall and smash it to pieces. If I smash the clock, I'll smash the TV next. I can't take the tantalizing, happy jazz music one second more.

Right as I'm about to free my hands, scream, take off a shoe and fling it hard at the TV, I hear a soft, angelic voice call my number. I look up and see a fat, conservatively dressed, middle-aged woman standing in a doorway. She smiles and motions me to follow her down a different corridor.

I rise from my chair and walk toward her, emotionless, as if I'm in a deep trance. She smiles again. She wouldn't smile if my test came back positive, I think. Or maybe she would. If she feels sorry for me, she'd smile.

With great effort, I follow her down the narrow hallway. My legs feel like two pillars of lead and don't want to budge. My heart is painful and pounding. I might have a massive heart attack in the middle of the hallway and die without ever knowing my test results.

I turn inside a tiny, bright office and stare, wide-eyed and dumb, at the woman. She introduces herself as an HIV health counselor. Unable to speak, I nod in response. She says a few more sentences that mean nothing to me when finally she says, "Your test is negative."

"It's negative? It is?" I whisper. I can feel the tears glistening in my eyes.

"Yes, it's negative," she repeats. "But this test isn't one hundred percent accurate and depending on when you might think you were exposed to the virus, you'll want to get retested."

I don't care about getting retested. As soon as I hear her say "negative," I feel the likes of a giant suction cup hovering above my head and sucking the anxiety out of my body. Instantly, I feel both exhausted and relieved. I'm overwhelmed with the urge to fall on my knees and praise God for giving me a second chance. I'm struck with the impulse to apologize to my parents and friends and beg for help and forgiveness. Don't let anyone tell you fear is a bad thing, ever, especially if it gets you back on the road to sanity.

The woman continues to blab on and on about HIV and prevention, but I don't listen. I'm negative and that's all that matters. I have a second chance. I learned a lesson the hard way, but not the hardest way. When she's done, I smile, thank her, hurry back down the narrow corridor and meet Amir.

"I'm negative!" I anxiously exclaim. My adrenaline is still running high from before. Amir half-smiles at me and starts walking toward the door. He's acting like he knew I was negative all along. I hear his stomach growl and figure he's hungry and wants to get something to eat.

Right as we head out the door, I grab his sweatshirt, turn him to face me and say, "I would never wish that one hour on anyone. Not anyone. Not ever."

He nods in agreement, when I remember he had a blood test too.

"By the way," I start as we walk to his car. "What was your result?"

"Negative," he answers in a distant, monotone voice. "Wouldn't it have been funny if it was Positive?"

I laugh as we exit the building. It's my first laugh of the day that doesn't feel forced. I can laugh freely now. I can smile now. I can do a lot of things now. My heart is full with a new kind of gratitude, a kind so strong that only comes after acute, traumatic experiences. I feel like I've slain the final dragon in Manic Kingdom and escaped. I have a second chance at life: a second chance to make my life work for me. It will take a lot of effort. I will struggle, and it won't be easy, but I am committed, I am grateful, and I never ever want to go back to Manic Kingdom. The fear of a return trip motivates me the most. A lot of good people don't get second chances, but I have one. Do you know what a second chance feels like after you almost threw everything away? Like it's the best thing in the world.

Epilogue

MANIC KINGDOM

One Year Later

"Should we meet you back at your apartment?" my mom asks as I unlock my Jeep in the packed parking lot of the Philadelphia Convention Center. It's the end of May and hot outside. I'm wearing a long black graduation gown and trying to hold my keys, phone, a gift from my sister, two bouquets of flowers and my newly received medical degree without dropping anything. It's my first official challenge as a new doctor. Consider it a cerebellum problem.

"I have to run somewhere, but I'll give you my keys and meet you there later," I say while loading up my Jeep. I just took a series of sweaty photos with my family and classmates, received hundreds of verbal congratulations and engaged in numerous painful repetitive conversations about my post-graduation plans. My face hurts from smiling. Now I just want to get out of this gown and away from everyone.

Don't get me wrong. I am soaring on the inside. I feel like a rock star. I can't wait to sign my first signature with "Doctor" in front of my name, especially after all I've been through, but I hate formal events and ceremonies. They're boring and mechanical and filled with cliché quotes and poems about success. I try to avoid them and would have preferred to get my diploma in the mail, but I know this ceremony was more for my family than me. After my breakdown, when the dean reaccepted me as a med student, I knew my entire family was holding their breath. Today they can officially breathe again.

My mom takes my apartment keys as I hop in my Jeep. "I won't be long," I say as I start the car, roll down the window and back out.

"Okay. We will see you in about an hour? And then we'll find a good Italian place for dinner? Not too late, Becka! We still have to drive home tonight, and your dad gets tired," my mom yells after me. I nod vigorously, hoping she'll interpret that as me agreeing with everything she said. I turn onto Franklin Street and head towards the freeway. I have a breezy half hour drive ahead of me.

I'm going to The Whitebrook Psychiatric Institution which is in a quiet suburb of Philadelphia. It is home to the chronically insane, including those deemed criminally insane. I plan on visiting Chase, whomI haven't seen in over a year. His parents told me that he has been at Whitebrook for around nine months. I talked to his social worker two weeks ago and asked her to ask Chase if I could visit. To my surprise, she called me back and said he'd love to see me. I'm nervous, but I'm also excited. I still care about him. I'm not sure if Chase knows that today is graduation day, or that it would have been his graduation day, too. Institutionalized folks tend to lose track of seasons and time. I'm not sure I'll even mention it, because I don't want to upset him. But I want to make sure I thank him, especially today. If it wasn't for him tutoring me in Gross Anatomy and dragging me to the lab to dissect and study dead people, I never would have made it. That was before he lost his mind, and before I lost my mind too. Unfortunately, only one of us got our minds back.

I have my mind back, at least for now. The thought alone makes me chuckle. As weird as this sounds, I feel like I'll always be in a rocky relationship with my mind. My mind is like the love of my life that I'm always afraid of losing. When it went away, I nearly crumbled. I was broken and useless, wandering around aimlessly searching for it. Now that it's back, I cater to it like a devoted, obsessed girlfriend. When my mind needs sleep, I sleep. When it needs food, I give it the best. When it needs a break, I go on a break. When it needs me to run, I run. The fear of losing it again is why I haven't lost it. A lot of people will say that fear is only destructive. I'm not one of them.

Fear is only natural after my experience with King. I could have been beaten, murdered or infected with a deadly disease. I could have lost my family, my career and eventually, he could have drugged me and made me a sex slave. The morbid possibilities are endless. To not feel fear would mean I'm dead.

I also feel loss. I haven't spoken to King since the day I left him, and I would be lying if I said I didn't sometimes miss him. I never want to be with him again, but I sometimes reminisce about our routine together. It's embarrassing to admit that fact, to myself and to the world, being that he's a rapist who cons women for a living. Missing him used to want to make me claw my skin off and bash my skull in. Gradually, with time, forgiveness and acceptance, I've come to believe that there is good and bad in everyone, including King, and missing the good in him doesn't mean I'm a bad or crazy person. It just means I was able to see the good.

King's in jail now. Not long after I left, he was arrested for assaulting a girl in the library. I Googled his name one day, and it showed up as a news story. I'm not sure how long he's in for, or how bad it was, but I'm assuming it's a long time. My guess is he'll go crazy not doing his routine.

Would you believe I still do bits of his routine? It plays

a significant role in my recovery. I move a lot because of King. He showed me that movement keeps me content and grounded. When I feel agitated or like I've been sitting too long, I get up and go for a walk or a run. I sleep with a yoga mat and a trampoline next to my bed, and I regularly do bear crawls as part of my workout. I still follow his sleep schedule. I go to sleep when it's dark and wake with the sunrise. Sleep should be another word for sanity. Because of him, I'm a minimalist. I only own and carry what I need. When I start to accumulate things, I feel cluttered and my mind becomes frenetic. So I throw away things I don't need. I don't eat raw meat or raw potatoes, but I keep my diet simple and organic. I avoid processed foods, snacks and keep alcohol, a depressant, to a minimum. I'm also off all medication. I can't blame drugs for my manic breakdown, as a lot of things were wrong with me, but I feel much better off of them. I suppose I'm recovered.

Recovery is a word I use cautiously. I prefer saying I'm trending upwards, because I still struggle. I have bad days and good days. When I have major setbacks, it scares me into thinking I'm headed towards the Manic Kingdom again. I cry, sometimes a lot. I'm still attracted to weird people, still date assholes, have passing suicidal thoughts, am overly sensitive, and question the meaning of everything. But the trend is upwards.

When people ask me how I bounced back, I shrug. The

truth is, I don't know. I don't know if it's something specific, like flipping a switch, or something more obscure and gradual. I made a lot of lifestyle changes that helped, but it could also be the passing of time, a change in perspective after a traumatic experience, a genetic manifestation, or finding a way to make medical school work for me. I didn't like the idea of being a traditional doctor in hospitals or clinics, where I felt like a temporary band aid for wounds that would never heal. Instead of giving it all up, I discovered the field of public health, which is about disease prevention and improving health on a population level. It felt like a fit. I found a fellowship in public health research, applied, got accepted and will start that program in August. I might still be depressed if I never found a career path that excited and inspired me. Think about it this way: we spend most of our lives at work. If we are depressed at work, then we are depressed most of our lives.

Damage control is a big part of recovery, too. I needed to take out more loans, ask my parents for financial help, downgrade into a smaller apartment and deal with painful rumors. I also had to apologize to a lot of people and convince the dean to give me a second chance. That was humiliating. I told him the gist of my story, but left out some of the juicer details. When you are attempting to bounce back from a breakdown, you may need to lie and embellish if you want a job or a school acceptance. People will claim not to judge you, but they will, often harshly, and very few people deserve to know everything about you. As cliché as this sounds, I also needed to learn how to love myself better. Every journey to self-love is unique, and I don't believe there is one true path. Some paths may involve therapy and self-help books, while other paths might include wise friends, life experiences, meditation, the belief in a higher power, or complete randomness. My path was eclectic, guided by two central themes: forgive myself for the mistakes I made and will continue to make and learn to know myself better. I don't regret anything about my childhood or life choices, but it is harder to know yourself when you are immersed in a controlling environment in which you are told what to do rather than having a choice, whether it is a strict upbringing, a religious school, the military or your place of employment. The true self gets buried in such an environment, and it's hard to love yourself when you don't even know yourself.

To love myself better I spent a lot of time alone, engaging in new experiences and embarking on new adventures while always being mindful of how I felt. I would practice choosing things that felt right for me and then work through any guilty feelings or opposition from my friends and family. It's an uncomfortable process and it's a life-long process, but it's well worth it. My eating disorder, depression and anxiety became less powerful on the path to self-love. Eventually I got to the point of not sacrificing my own wishes to please others or to uphold an ideal image of me. Approval-seeking is the opposite of self-love. If I was to define self-love, I'd say it is the act of saying yes to the things I want to say yes to and saying no to the things I want to say no to. At least that's what it feels like to me.

Someone asked me to write a self-help book about depression and recovery, but I declined. I would feel like an imposter. I'm no guru on the subject, and I don't know if it was one thing, a combination of things, or pure luck that caused me to feel better. No one knows. It's all a mystery. Self-help books are honest gestures but a lot of speculation, and I don't want to speculate.

I shake my head, pull up to a red light and wait. Whitebrook is one left turn away. The institution looks surprisingly friendly, a stark comparison to the many that look like they belong in horror movies. A red brick building looms in front of me. There are bars on the windows, but that's expected. The building is surrounded by lush green lawns, flower beds and tall healthy trees. Birds are chirping as I walk in the main door to check in at the front desk.

After signing in, a receptionist tells me that Chase will be waiting in the visitors' area, which is located on the ward. A guard motions me to follow him and we walk down several long marble hallways to a locked door. He swipes a card against a sensor, the door buzzes and we walk inside. A tired-looking woman hugging a clipboard greets us on the other side.

"Hi. Follow me to the visitors' area," she says matter-of-factly.

I follow her down the hallway, glancing nervously in all different directions. There are a few patients ambling about. They move sluggishly and look heavily sedated, like they've been here forever. The clipboard lady ushers me inside a bland room with a few round tables, plastic chairs and two worn leather couches. Chase is sitting on one of the chairs with his elbows on the table and his fists holding up his chin. His face looks bloated, huge, like a full moon. He's wearing a loose-fitting blue t-shirt, but I can tell he gained a lot of belly weight too. I assume he's heavily medicated, since weight gain is a common side effect of the drugs. His eyes look calm yet faded, as if all the color was sucked out. He sees me and smirks. We're off to a friendly start, I think. I sit down in an adjacent chair and lightly touch his shoulder.

"Chase, hi! It's been a while, huh?" I say while trying to hide my nervousness with a smile.

"You have fifteen minutes," the clipboard lady states flatly and walks out.

"Ha," Chase starts then laughs, "It has. You look great. How are you?"

"I'm good. I'm really good. Moses is good. She misses you and wanted me to say hi."

Chase smiles when he hears her name.

"I didn't know she learned English. Always knew she was smart," Chase jokes. I giggle in response while racking my brain for ways to continue a conversation.

"How...how are you?"

"Well, I'm in here. That's not ideal. I'm on a lot of medication, but you probably knew that just by looking at me. I gained like 50 pounds," Chase says.

I nod in response. "Has your family been by to visit?"

"Not much. My parents are older, you know. It's tough for them."

"I know. I'm sure they would if they could. Um, do you feel...better? Do you think they are helping you in here?"

Chase lets out a bitter laugh and says, "No. I mean, no one is being an asshole. They're nice. The food is institution food, but it could be worse. What about you? Are you better?"

I'm not sure how to answer or what he's referring to. He couldn't possibly know about King or that I left school and had a mini-breakdown. I decide to keep it simple and play along.

"I am. I'm doing really well."

Chase smiles. "That's good. Really good."

An awkward silence takes over the conversation as Chase looks away and stares blankly at the far wall. I start biting my nails while trying to think about harmless things to talk about. Nothing is coming to mind so I decide to do what I came to do, which is to thank him.

"Chase," I start. "You know all those nights you dragged me to the Gross lab? And how you used to tutor me in the apartment? Remember how much I hated that stuff?"

"I do," he murmurs distantly.

"I just want to tell you that you helped me so much. I never would have made it through without you. Thank you for that."

Chase smiles, but doesn't say anything. Another painful moment of silent awkwardness ensues, and this time Chase breaks it. "Did you graduate today?" he asks. I feel my eyebrows raise. I guess he does know about graduation.

"I did, yeah," I say. It feels bittersweet to respond. Suddenly, I feel sad.

"Congratulations, doctor!" Chase exclaims with perhaps sarcasm or maybe bitterness. I can't tell.

I simply nod. I can feel my eyes welling up with tears as I silently coach myself out of crying. Crying in front of Chase cannot happen. That could stir him up in a very bad way.

"Becka," Chase says and clears his throat. "I need your help. I need to know where you got the electronics that were in our apartment."

I get an instant adrenaline rush that causes me to perk up. Did I really just hear him ask me about electronics? Is he still delusional? I thought the medication would have stopped the psychosis. He's clearly taking it; he's huge and yet it's not helping?

"What?" I practically whisper.

He starts to squirm in his chair and his upper body starts quivering. His faded eyes narrow with agitation. I swallow hard, wondering if I just poked the dragon.

"Becka, now you have the chance. I have PTSD because of what you did to me, Becka. I could have had you arrested, but I knew you wouldn't have become a doctor if I did. You brought in new electronics once a month. I Googled them and saw that they were all hidden cameras. I know you weren't up to this by yourself, Becka, so who put you up to it?"

I'm speechless. All I can do is stare and remind myself that the exit door is only a few feet away. I did not prepare for this.

"Becka," Chase starts. His voice is loud and desperate. "Please. Please tell me. I have been violated. I lost everything. Now is your chance to help someone who has been violated. Take it or leave it. Where, Becka, did you get those electronics?"

I stare at Chase without uttering a word. The sudden adrenaline rush, my sweaty palms, him interrogating me and my inability to get through to him all send me back to our shared apartment. He's not better. He's still sick. The real him is gone, and I'm talking to a ghost.

Chase stares past me at the wall again. He's shaking more violently now. I slide out of my chair, scurry to the door and walk out. I speed-walk towards the guard who buzzes me out without asking any questions. A tear rolls down my cheek, and I wipe it away. Just walk, I tell myself. I don't regret my Irish goodbye. I don't know how to say goodbye in situations like that.

Outside, in the parking lot, I take a few deep breaths. I'm relieved to be out of there. I scurry to my Jeep, hop in and start driving back to Philly. I turn on the radio, roll down the window and drive.

The music is blaring, but I barely notice it. I think about Chase. I think about his moon-shaped head and angry eyes. I wonder what medication he's taking, and why he's still delusional. I thought he'd be doing better. Now that I've seen him, I'll be more prepared next time. I won't have to run out on him and be overwhelmed by confusion and sadness. I'll have answers ready and show him that I'm his friend. I won't give up.

That's just it. There's hope for some people and no hope for others. It's our humanity that causes us to not give up on either.

About the Author

Erin Stair, MD, MPH, resides in New York City and runs BloomingWellness.com, a holistic health website, blog and wellness store. She is the creator of ZENBands and ZENTones, natural tools for stress and anxiety. To write her, learn more about her, or sign up for her newsletter, visit www.Bloomingwellness.com.

Manufactured by Amazon.ca
Bolton, ON

11147810R00162